THE POSTMODERN CATHOLIC

Living in an inverted,
alternative universe

THE POSTMODERN CATHOLIC

Living in an inverted,
alternative universe

Fr. Dale Tupper

Leonine Publishers
Phoenix, Arizona

Copyright © 2020 Fr. Dale Tupper

All rights reserved. No part of this book may be reproduced or transmitted in any form or by any means, electronic or mechanical, including photocopying, recording, or by any information storage or retrieval system now existing or to be invented, without written permission from the respective copyright holder(s), except for the inclusion of brief quotations in a review.

Published by
Leonine Publishers LLC
Phoenix, Arizona, USA

ISBN-13: 978-1-942190-61-5

Library of Congress Control Number: 2020914007

10 9 8 7 6 5 4 3 2 1

Visit us online at www.leoninepublishers.com
For more information: info@leoninepublishers.com

Table of Contents

Foreword vii

Part I

The Context We Have Inherited

1. Contemporary Crosscurrents 3
2. The Empty Container of Secularism 11
3. The Contrasting Image: The Blood of the Chalice . . 17
4. Fifty Years. 21
5. Cascading Dominoes 27
6. The Secret We Have: The Risen Christ 41
7. Oxygen Level Critical 47

Part II

The Mass We Celebrate

8. The Spiritual Dimension of the Mass 55
9. A Diamond in a Bed of Gravel 63
10. The Dimensions of the Mass 71
11. The Extent of the Silence 81
12. The Bread of the Eucharist 87
13. The Moment to Which and from Which
    All Flows 93
14. What Happens to Us in the Mass? 101

15. Fathers and Sons: Reaching into the Central
    Moment 111
16. Unrequited Love 121
17. Time, Upended 129

Part III

The Opportunities We Have

18. Hidden in Plain Sight 137
19. The Question the World Is Afraid to Ask 143
20. At the Crossroads 151
21. Nothingness and Death 155
22. What Has Changed? 165
23. Goodness 175
24. Without Christ, with Christ 183
25. The Eventual Meeting with Christ 193
26. There Is No Other 199
27. Analogies for Our Times 209
28. On the Importance of Our Sins 217
29. Hearing the Voice from Beyond 221
30. Identity and Our Souls 227
31. The Choice We Have 235
32. The Milieu in Which We Live 243
33. The Need to Stay Awake 253

A Partial Bibliography 259
Some Additional Notes on the Content 263

Foreword

Catholics of the 21st century are having to live within Satan's inverted, alternative universe, often times without the tools to either comprehend the context, or to endure the chaos that has resulted from this upside-down, inside-out universe.

Where did this new and strange environment of the 21st century come from? How are we to identify exactly what this milieu is? How does our Catholicism cope with both the assault that it is, and the delusions that form its essence? We need to talk directly about the post-modern world, this secular era, nailing exactly what it is and what it is doing to the lives of Catholics, former Catholics, and the lost souls that make up this dramatic new time.

We also need a response to the confusion, something that we can center ourselves around that will sustain us. That center, I believe, is the Mass. If we enter deeply enough into the Mass, we will find that it gives us all we need, not only a defense against this era, but it will fill us with a spirit of joy and peace, even in the midst of this inverted, alternative universe of Satan.

The Last 50 Years

No era, short of the Reformation, has seen more changes in the priesthood or in the Catholic Church than in the last fifty years. At least three times, it appears as if we have experienced a paradigm shift in the Church, first, from the immigrant Church I grew up in, in the

1940s and 50s, then, from Vatican II at the time I was ordained, and now, as things have once more shifted to a Catholicism in an age of total secularization.

I offer these thought experiments, culled from those fifty years within the parish priesthood, fifty years of an interactive triangle of prayer, reading, and preaching, joined to fifty years of struggling with trying to understand what is happening in these times. My hope is that poetics might overcome any deficiencies of my spirituality or my theology.

There are a lot of things that this writing is not about. I have written these essays or thought experiments not as a formal theology, even if there is theology within it. I am a parish priest with fifty years' experience, with no other qualifications that I can bring to bear.

This also means that I am not an expert in theological ways. I am simply an individual priest living in the midst of rapidly changing times, times which often appear to me to be unique in the last two thousand years, times which seem to defy explanation and remain incomprehensible except from a faith perspective.

Numerous resources have said that it was the 1960s that constituted the watershed moment in our American culture. As it happened, I entered the seminary in the fall of 1959 and was ordained in 1967. Looking back now, it seems like that might have been some really bad timing!

When I have gotten together with some of my former seminary classmates, some of them were still trying to piece together what happened to their vocation, that they never got to the priesthood, or that they left the priesthood shortly after ordination. The decade of the 60s disrupted and destabilized a great deal of our assumptions and values of those times. In addition, these fifty years have left a lot of our experiences incomprehensible.

For those of us who remained, it often looks as if we are a part of a shattered priesthood, wounded from all that happened. However, it has also been a holy priesthood, one rich in simplicity and humility, requiring a lot of faith and trust in God's plan. Simplicity and humility have been among the primary traits required to be a disciple of Christ working in the Church in these times.

Perhaps it was not so unfortunate to have been here for these fifty years. It was clearly a time of purification, a kind of extended Lent, both for the priesthood and for the Church. I am proud to have been a part of it all. I offer these words with a grateful heart, in the hope that they will be for the greater honor and glory of God.

Planting Oak Trees

Here is a concluding image regarding what my hope is in this writing. My grandfather, born sometime around the 1880s, was a farmer, living in southeastern Minnesota. However, at some point, probably well before the 1920s, he came down with tuberculosis. At that time, medicine was not so advanced. Penicillin and other such medicines were not readily available to treat such a disease as tuberculosis, and it took my grandfather from the farming that he loved. The Mayo Clinic told him in about 1940 that he probably had only a year left to live. He died in 1954.

Fortunately he had six sons who could pick up what he could no longer do. Eventually he reached the point where all he could do was walk around the farm on his good days. He also took occasional walks through the valley where his farm house was built.

On those walks he would take a bag of acorns and walk with his cane, dropping the acorns on the ground, and using his cane to press them into the soil, in the hope of keeping them away from the squirrels. In time, he saw the results of the planting of acorns that he had done.

Some hundred years later, when you drive through that little valley, there is this forest of oak trees that has come to full growth, filling the valley with diversity and completion. It was the only thing left that the tuberculosis would allow him to do. I don't know if he had any expectations about his simple planting effort, but the yield was far and above what he imagined.

My hope in these times of secularism, in this era of Satan's inverted, alternative universe, is that we might have the same hope and optimism that what we plant in this era may come to fruition, as much as my grandfather's oak trees did.

At root, I believe that there resides, within the Mass that we celebrate, enough to bring our Catholic Faith to fruition in some later days, long after we are gone.

Thus, my target audience, should this writing find circulation whatsoever, is whoever is Catholic and might be seeking validation for the Faith they have been given. I seek not to evangelize beyond that, assuming that the Holy Spirit will form and shape the Catholic of the present in some of the ways that I hold precious, and thus reach out solidly and firmly to those victimized by the secularism of these times. I believe that we can go from acorns to oak trees, in that Spirit.

In Thanksgiving

My gratitude to those who have assisted me along this journey of writing, a journey that I did not intentionally seek to begin, a journey I still do not know exactly to where or to what it will lead.

I am especially appreciative of those who sat and listened to my homilies over the years. By their listening they schooled me in what they especially needed to hear. I could recognize what it was to which they were especially attentive. Their attentiveness schooled me as well in my spirituality and theology, in ways my formal education never did. I'm sure this writing is in many ways the result of that schooling.

My thanks to those who assisted me in this writing, by offering their input, and by their careful scrutiny of the text, especially Fr. James Steffes, Louise Stemp, and Sr. Jane Weisgram. A special thanks to Mr. Thomas Miller, who has led me to take additional steps to the circulation of this material.

Part I

The Context We Have Inherited

1. Contemporary Crosscurrents

That you may be blameless and innocent, children of God without blemish in the midst of a crooked and perverse generation, among whom you shine like lights in the world.
Philippians 2:14-15

When I was a seminarian, in theology school some 50-plus years ago, I heard that if you wanted to understand what was happening at the Vatican II Council meetings, and where the Church was going to go in the future, you needed to be able to read the theologians of the day in French or German. None of it was translated into English, and none of us read French or German. We were not the bright lights of the future!

However, about 10 years ago I had my chance. I found by coincidence that those translations had now been made, and I could start to read those authors, called the Communio group of theologians. I started to read and to wonder more deeply about the questions that I had. What was the real origin of that council? What was the underlining issue driving it? What was the context behind it all? Where is this all going for the Church and our world?

It began for me with a few days of vacation, and I decided to visit museums in Washington D.C. On a whim, I thought that I should also visit the National Shrine at Catholic University while I was there, a kind of bow to my heritage. While there I discovered their bookstore, rich with the authors of that Communio group. I brought some home, and then began to read. I believe that it was the hand of the Spirit that led me to that moment. It was something of an awakening. I could understand what I was reading, and it was not beyond my abilities, after many years in the priesthood. I found that their thoughts translated into good homilies. People told me so.

My reading kept leading me to other authors, pushing me back in history, allowing me to find others who had been writing from a sound, Catholic perspective. It has been probably one of the richest times in my life, for which I am ever grateful. It pushed me to new levels of understanding. I was walking through a garden of wonders that I hadn't perceived before. Whole pieces of the mystery fell into place for me, much of it beyond words.

The Crosscurrent on the Surface

It has also filled in some answers for me, regarding the times in which we live. For all the time of my priesthood, now over fifty years, I have been watching crosscurrents interacting with each other.

One of those has been the continual contraction of Faith in our culture. I used to say to myself: "Why do we seem to be losing this fight? We are supposed to be the bearers of Good News for the world. Doesn't anybody want what the Gospel has to offer?" I had thought that social justice and peace issues would light the way for our world to come to Christ, that these things would ratchet the world into the kingdom, as a kind of incremental eschatology.

However, everywhere I looked, secularism was on the rise, the existence of God denied and the presence of

Christ ignored in a sort of functional atheism. Children seemed to be less and less at the center of the family, and marriage seemed more and more a thing of the past. Now identity politics seems to redefine everything about gender and sexuality. Everything about secularism and the postmodern world seems pointed toward a kind of tragic defeat of faith. Peace and justice seem a fugitive in our day. The Church looks like the odd man in this picture, irrelevant, squarely beyond the times, hopelessly protesting in words nobody can hear.

A Crosscurrent Below the Radar

The other crosscurrent has been what was happening below the radar in the Church. My witness of the missions in the growth of the Korean church, watching it rise from the ashes of the Korean War into a church of vitality and strength.

Then there was my experience of starting a parish from scratch, and seeing it flower from some source of power beyond me, filled with young couples, lots of baptisms, and the energy to build a parish and school from nothing, with parishioners willing to make major sacrifices to make it happen.

Then there was my journey to an established parish, brimming with Hispanic children and young couples and their discovery of the Neo-catechumenal Way, and how it brought youth to the Gospel and families to Christ.

All of this has been unseen, below the radar, and prophetic of what is to come, a witness of the Holy Spirit in our times, ignored by the media, disbelieved by the majority. This piece of our contemporary times lies hidden from our secular culture, belonging only to us, sheltered by God's love, invisible except to the eyes of faith. It is truly below the radar.

The Vatican Council

I have also discerned the grief of the Church in the 20th century, as it witnessed two major wars and the loss of countless lives, not to speak of the ongoing, undeclared wars such as Yugoslavia, Vietnam, Iraq, and Afghanistan, among others. In all of these, I believe that a key moment of the 20th century was the Holocaust, the murder of the Jewish people by the Nazis. How could we, who are Christians, who are committed to Jesus Christ have participated through a kind of passive neglect in the murder of six-million innocents, Jews who are the chosen people of God? They were our brothers. Where were we? What went wrong? Where was our Christianity?

Why wasn't the Gospel deeper in our hearts that supposed Catholics would have actively or passively participated in such evil? I believe this to be the root of the call of the post-Vatican II Church for re-evangelization, that calls for a renewal in a far deeper way than we had mistakenly set out from the first days after the Council, misunderstanding the call of the Spirit to us, thinking that the change could be done with newly translated texts.

In those times, we all participated in a set of compromises with the secularism around us that we thought was somehow going to win over those we wanted to have come home, or to stay home. We were the Neville Chamberlains of the post-Vatican II Church, thinking that we could bargain with the culture of the times, as Chamberlain had done with Hitler and Nazi Germany about Czechoslovakia. They took what we gave them, and then asked for more. They cleverly turned identity politics into a new human right, with only the word of Congress and the courts.

We thought we could win them over. How naive we were!

By now we ought to have the sense that this is not going to stop. We know this journey is not over. We have long since reached the end of any compromises, but we know that continuing membership in this culture will expect more. The secularism of our times will aggressively and definitively demand more participation in the emptiness of Satan's inverted, alternative universe.

After all, everything that we hold precious, secularism sees as an affront to the direction it wants everything to go. Secularism will have to insist on our participation!

The Gospel for the 21st Century

The demands of the Gospel in these times are a thousand times deeper than our original assumptions. Today demands a response focused totally on the presence of the risen Christ in our midst and total conversion of heart, so deep that we would be willing to die for it, and that we would give our lives every day to make it happen. The aggressiveness of American secularism is awakening us little by little to the new level of commitment that is necessary for these times.

One of my discoveries in all of this has been the depth of the Mass, and the extent to which the faithful are willing to dedicate themselves in the mystery of the Mass. I know, shame on me, for not knowing this from the beginning, for not thinking it through sooner.

The silence at homily time tells me that the faithful yearn for a true spiritual knowledge of the mysteries that surround the Mass. I find that they can't get enough of how God's love works, how far Christ went, out of love for them, and how the Eucharist opens a pathway to the eternal, lived now in this world. They are repeatedly astounded that the presence of Christ is pinned to their lives in a most real way. It is almost as if I can say these same things over and over, and there is something within that they need to hear that they can't get enough of. They always seem to be listening as if they were hearing it for the first time. The truth of these things shared is stunning!

The Mass for the 21st Century

I see the Mass as the ultimate antidote for anyone seeking to understand and to cope with the darkness and emptiness, the chaos and hopelessness of this secular world. The mysteries of the Eucharist open a doorway of meaning and understanding for anyone who seeks to live the faith fully in the midst of the confusion of these times.

There has been a kind of studied indifference to the Mass for the past couple of generations. You celebrated the Eucharist, and then got on to whatever it was that was important that day — no more the undiscovered cornerstone of it all. This postmodern world, this empty container of secularism, this inverted, alternative universe of Satan demands the most fundamental response possible.

That response can only be our undivided attention to what the central moment of the Eucharist is: the moment of total self-giving on the part of Christ for us, in an absolute self-sacrifice to the Father for each of us and all of humanity. This moment is not just another moment, rather it is *the* moment, the foundational moment of all that we are and are to become. It is nothing short of how we are to deal with what this world has become. It defines who and what we are to become today, a total union with Christ as children of the Father.

Putting the Focus on Christ, Totally

At this moment in time, we are Peter getting out of the boat to walk toward Jesus at His very invitation. Everything around us swirls in chaos. As long as we hold the focus on Christ in His moment of self-giving we shall do fine. It was not just Jesus of Nazareth that Peter was to hold before his eyes, it was the Christ, about to journey to Jerusalem in obedience to His Father, to give Himself in exchange for us in an act of total poverty and humility, the very moment we celebrate timelessly and from sunrise to sunset, east to west, in the Eucharist.

Peter, at that moment on the Sea of Galilee, could not have known then what we now know. Ours is a post-Easter vision encapsulated in the Mass, a sustaining vision, designed for walking toward our redeemer, on whatever water that swirls around us, whatever winds that furiously assault us. We now know that Peter's Jesus is truly the risen Christ, coming toward us now, hidden but visible, in the very transcendental moment of the Mass that we are to carry throughout the day and the moments of our lives.

2. The Empty Container of Secularism

> They cannot scare me with their empty spaces
> Between stars — on stars where no human race is.
> I have it in me so much nearer home
> To scare myself with my own desert places.
> "Desert Places," by Robert Frost

These essays, or if you will, these thought experiments are about the contrast between two analogies. This contrast is the critical choice for our times, especially for the Catholic. The first analogy is that of an empty container.

Visualize an empty plastic container, cracked and transparent, without any contents. This is an analogy for the secularism of our times, the postmodern world in which we reside. This container is empty simply because its major premise is that God is dead, that there is no God whatsoever. As a result, the secularism of our times consists of a void. Nothing has replaced God. Nothingness is the result. To put it another way, if not nothingness, then there is just us, alone in the universe and without purpose.

It seems to me that they probably should have thought about what was to replace the God that they jettisoned, but they didn't. It certainly should have been something other than just the "self"!

The ancient and medieval worlds understood reality as a kind of chain of being. There was God, then the angels, then humanity, next the animals, and finally the inanimate objects, the things of the world at the lowest level. God dwelt above the chain. Evil resided somewhat below, as the negation of this chain, bearing an uncanny resemblance to the secularism that has been created.

Once God was eliminated, humanity became the center of things, God became an afterthought and was soon disposed of. Now there is supposed to be only us as secular, alone in Satan's inverted, alternative universe, and in essence, that's a really scary, empty space.

The New Norm for the 21st Century

The world now considers this secularism the norm for the 21st century. However, this way of the world is a statement of what is not, rather than what is. This absence is anything but normal. How delusional to let an absence define who and what we are to be today!

In the 15th century, people thought that the earth was the center of the universe. Copernicus redefined things by suggesting that the sun was the center, not the earth. It was a shocking theory then: "What? We are not the center of things?"

It seems that secularism has now reversed Copernicus. By dispatching God, humanity is now back at the center, albeit, in a kind of an uncomfortable center in a meaningless, endless universe.

Put another way, once humanity prayed the Lord's Prayer: "Thy will be done." Now there's nothing but "me" at the center of this secular universe, so humanity ends up saying: "My own will be done; no God is going to tell me what to do." The "I" is back at the center, by default, by elimination, by desire.

A Massive Redefinition

Secularism requires a massive redefinition of life that has not yet succeeded in replacing this chain of being, which only faith in Jesus Christ and God the Father can illuminate. The chain of being only makes sense if there is a creator and ultimately, a redeemer.

Right at the core of this postmodern way of life is the problem of death itself. The closer one comes to death, the more weight the life we have takes on, and the more monstrous death looks to the secular world. If we are all we have, if we are nothing but ourselves, with no source, our existence becomes a distorted need, redefining everything else in the world around the avoidance of death. No wonder we place such high demands on medicine today; we absolutely have to go on living in this world, as there is nothing else!

Further, there seems no explanation, no compensation for the injustices and wrongs that happen in this world. "After all, there is nothing but this." If this is all there is, what about suffering? There is no explanation here. What about death among the young and innocent? Again there is no explanation here. You can't even blame God, as he doesn't exist anymore! No wonder secularism loves assisted suicide: you can milk life for what you can get, then pull the plug.

Absent any meaning or purpose in this new normal, plain-old regular suicide will do. Without a transcendent theology, there is simply no meaning or purpose intrinsic to life. This is the greatest emptiness of secularism, and it haunts the postmodern world. Clearly no one can cope for very long without some intrinsic meaning to their existence. Yet, that is what the postmodern world proposes.

The Absence of Meaning in Secularism

It is curious that in secularism the absence of meaning is coupled with the abhorrence of death. They are in contradiction to each other. If there is no meaning, why not death. Meaning disarms death, shrinking its dimension in our lives.

Meaning in our Christianity centers on our relationship to Christ. We know who and what we are, in relation to the God who created us, and to the Christ who redeemed us. We know where we are going, and we know the cross of Christ will get us there. We can endure anything when we know we possess the love of Christ. Last of all, we have the certain knowledge that death is simply the doorway to new life.

However, if you have removed God, scrubbed him away, deleted him as nonexistent, how could there be any intrinsic meaning to this existence. One existentialist, Camus, came up with only one thing: to live with courage in a meaningless world. That amounts, in my mind, to a pretty paltry sense of meaning for which to grasp.

Another area of difficulty for secularism is that there seems to be no design to this world. This is so, despite all the science around us that keeps finding order and all the mathematics that can find such elegant proofs for this universe. Yet, there appears no intelligent design, no direction other than a senseless drift of evolution. If I am going to choose secularism, there will be nothing intrinsic to whatever patterns we see, only random chance. You can't have it both ways. Either there is design, coming from somewhere, or there is not.

In addition there is no destiny, only the now, the empty sequence of events that is in reality going nowhere. This world seems to be made for some sort of order, yet there is none except by doing a kind of "selfie" to create a memory. There is nothing intrinsic to a world without God, a world of secularism, a postmodern time, where everything definable has come off its hinges. It's a day at a time, without direction or purpose, lurching any which way.

In the end, all that would be left in a secular world, carried to its conclusion, would be sexual expression and greed as a purpose for living. In fact, given our times, it looks as if that conclusion is already upon our world. Nothing goes beyond this life. There is no sin, no need for forgiveness, no accounting for what we do or do not do in this life. It all ends with death. Period. Take, get, and enjoy. Then, quit!

The secularism of our times is truly an empty container, holding nothing, a transparent, cracked plastic pitcher that will never be filled with anything but what the individual can scrape up within his or her lifetime. Even then, it all leaks out in the end. It holds nothing.

I suspect Robert Frost in his poem, "Desert Places," already sensed where this world was going and couldn't help but fear then the hollowness of our time that was yet to come.

> And lonely as it is, that loneliness
> Will be more lonely ere it will be less —
> A blanker whiteness of benighted snow
> With no expression, nothing to express.

3. The Contrasting Image: The Blood of the Chalice

> So the soldiers came and broke the legs of the first and then of the other one who was crucified with Jesus. But when they came to Jesus and saw that he was already dead, they did not break his legs, but one soldier thrust his lance into his side, and immediately blood and water flowed out.
> John 19:32-33

Come now into a different world, the world of the Blood of the Chalice. If the world of the secular is an empty container, the world of the Blood of the Chalice is the opposite. The Blood of the Chalice is a world laden with meaning and symbol, inundated with analogy, saturated with the inexhaustible, flowing river of Christ's love. It is precisely that meaning that is contained within the Eucharist.

From the very beginning, the Last Supper, this Chalice of Blood contained everything that would ever be expressed regarding the love of God for us. Liturgically, the Mass, the Eucharist is the central event that characterizes this new life that has come to us from the cross. The blood and water flowing from the side of Christ enriches and completes the soul of every person who has given his or her self over to Christ.

I can think of no change in the liturgy from Vatican II that means more than the restoration of the Blood of Christ for all the faithful at the moment of Communion. We know that for centuries, it was the celebrant alone who received the Blood of Christ. Perhaps it was a difficulty in logistics. Perhaps the times were just not ready for this option. Then, too, not that many received the Body of Christ, other than on an annual Easter experience. The Church has worked for centuries to make Communion an event at every Eucharist for both clergy and lay, the final step done, by allowing the Blood of Christ for the entire community in post-Vatican II days.

The Body and Blood of Christ

To receive the Body of Christ is an awesome experience, beyond what we can grasp in the moment. That Christ Himself would come to us as a spiritual food is a miracle beyond miracle. It remains almost incomprehensible that Christ would do this for us, and that He actually comes into our soul and resides there when we receive Him, and that He extends the very moment of our reconciliation in the cross with God into the present. I suspect that we first have to sense the sacred importance of receiving the Body of Christ, and only then can we appreciate the Blood of Christ.

However, I believe that the Blood of Christ takes this mystery of the Eucharist a step deeper. Blood is different than body, more intense, more personal, in a sense even more risky. Even in these modern, medical times, blood still represents life itself in an almost sacramental way, even before it becomes the Blood of Christ. The ancient Hebrew sense that blood equals life is still very much a part of the mystery of life itself, even apart from the Blood of Christ. Often we are shocked to see a wound, with blood flowing. We are surprised especially by our own blood, flowing out of us at the moment of an injury. It seems almost as if it is the life within us that is flowing out.

One of the most striking connections we have in the Mass is that the Blood of Christ that we are receiving is the very blood flowing from the side of Christ on the cross that John is talking about in his Gospel. That puts our connection in direct contact with that moment on the cross. Like ourselves, that blood flowing out of the side of Christ is the very life of Christ itself flowing out into our lives.

This blood flowing from the side of Christ is the blood that resides in the chalice of the Eucharist. Two thousand years are absorbed at the moment of Eucharist, and we are right there ourselves at that sanctifying moment of the cross.

Could we possibly be any more distant from the empty container of secularism? In the Blood of the Chalice we connect the cross and the now, reaching across this world into the next, uniting ourselves with each other and with everyone else who has tasted the Blood of Christ, living or deceased.

Twofold Consequences of the Eucharist

The Blood of the Chalice flows directly from the side of Christ to us. There is no distance between the moment of the lance entering the side of Christ and the moment of the Eucharist. There is no distance of time or place.

The Blood of the Chalice is transformative. To receive the Blood of the Chalice attentively and sincerely is to allow the Blood of Christ to flow deeply into our souls, to orient our lives and hearts to what Christ would have us be. Meaning and purpose, destiny and identity all fall into place for us. All of a sudden, in the Blood of Christ we can see with clarity where we have come from, what we have gained, why we are here, and where we are going.

If anyone takes Communion this way, by receiving the Blood of the Chalice, that act illuminates definitively, first, the awesome grace poured out to us, and second, underscores the emptiness of the secularism of our times. Never, upon realizing what it is that we have received, could we return to live that empty, causeless and hopeless way of the 21st century.

In fact, it is not our faith that is the crisis in these times. The Blood of Christ with us establishes once and for all the foundation that we have in Christ. In truth, it is secularism alone that is fraught with inconsistencies and contradictions. Secularism is clearly in an endless downward spiral. I believe that secularism is an instrument of Satan's alternative, inverted universe, one devoid of mystery and truth, one without the love that only the risen Christ possesses and then shares with His brothers and sisters. We need not mistake the crisis of secularism to be our crisis, because we have the antidote, the Blood of Christ.

Finally, it is not an accident that this mystery is hidden from those on the outside. It is simply too much for this world, just as it was for the crowd when Jesus announced that eternal life depended on eating His Body and drinking His Blood.

The Blood of Christ is reserved for those who have found already the presence of Christ within them. The Blood of the Chalice is reserved for those who have been taken into the mystery. It is the last, great mystery that a neophyte, the catechumen experiences when they have just been taken into the assembly through the waters of baptism. It remains the last, great mystery for each of us who come to the Eucharist. There is no mystery for this world above the mystery of the Blood of the Chalice. The Blood of the Chalice is the absolute illumination of the disciples of Christ.

4. Fifty Years

Jesus came to Galilee proclaiming the gospel of God: "This is the time of fulfillment. The kingdom of God is at hand."
Mark 1:15

There is a scene in the film *Titanic* where, having struck the iceberg, the ship's leadership gathered with the ship architect to learn that the Titanic was indeed sinking. When asked, "How much time do we have?" the architect responded, "About two hours." Silence followed.

I do not know what iceberg our postmodern world has struck, or even when our world will flounder, but I do know that for my fifty years of priesthood, I have been keenly aware of a similar intuition about the future. The feeling was with me virtually from the first days of my priesthood.

Fifty years, of course, is a lot longer than two hours. However, given the two thousand years of the Church, fifty years is just a drop, more of the equivalent of an earthquake than the movement of a glacier. Still, I find myself shocked by the suddenness of change that I have witnessed.

Catholic Schools Then and Now

There were 150 ninth graders, in five sections of religion classes. It was 1967. There were no vetted textbooks, no assignments, no grades, no curriculum. I was grateful that there were even desks in the classroom. Instead just these ninth graders who had been told that everything was changing, and that the new was just around the corner. I created curriculum day after day, hoping that some useful theology would emerge.

By the end of the year, I knew all I had going for me was the patience and tolerance of the hundred and fifty, and that was mighty thin. I knew deep in my heart that it was not simply a matter of textbooks. It was that nothing I did got to the kernel of truth that would bring about conversion of heart in the lives of those students.

For four more years, I struggled to find what exactly would have the results that I knew were needed. There was nothing. I got better at curriculum and at the profession of teaching, but the essence of what lay at the root of our Faith I could not convey and there was little to help me. I could not turn the final corner of theology to evangelize the youth I was working with in a definitive manner.

I now know that I was defeated, not just by my flawed theology, but by the emerging universe of our burgeoning secular world. Even then, before cell phones and computers, these students already had been evangelized by the music, television, and film, and by a new spirit of something that was being released in our times that essentially disarmed and undermined the personal ownership of the presence of Christ in their lives. It was the 1960s.

From teaching, I was sent to be an administrator, moving from one school to another, and then another. Nothing in each of those schools was enough to turn the students to being fully Catholic in today's world. Again, we were outnumbered by the shifting culture, this time mixing drugs and alcohol in plentiful amounts to the behavior of youth. Clearly the family was shifting as well. Before, parents would side with the school regarding their children's behaviors. Later, they would side with their children over against the school. Threats of lawsuits were common. It was then the 1970s.

The Coming Confrontation

And so, the erosion continued, shrinking the footprint of the Gospel in the culture of our land. There was that uneasy feeling that theology and faith in these times was no longer necessary, even more that it simply didn't make any sense to more and more of the population.

Fifty years later, the erosion continues, intensified. At the same time, we have learned, learned a great deal. We now have nothing but that central kernel of the presence of the risen Christ in our midst, especially in the Eucharist. The nihilism promised long ago by Friedrich Nietzsche that God is dead now rules. Virtue and morality now consists of broken fragments and of shifting sands of irrationality, floating aimlessly at the will of whatever group predominates.

Years after being ordained a priest, I learned that the roots of the Vatican Council were grounded in the memory of the wars of the 20th century. Estimates of the deaths as a result of those two great wars numbered in the millions and millions. No figure I've seen has been definitive, somewhere between thirty and sixty million deaths just in the Second World War. In the midst of that, six million Jews were murdered in the concentration camps of the Nazis. The fallout was immense.

The question after these wars had to do with what went wrong in the consciousness of Christians that allowed such atrocities to have occurred, when every teaching of Jesus Christ is opposed to violence, and almost every country where there was such violence were supposedly Christian. Where did we fail in our faith?

Clearly something had been missing in the faith and the baptisms in the Church at those times. Should we have not been alert in those days to what was coming? When it came, each of those two twentieth-century wars, it must have been like the moment on the Titanic. "How much time do we have? About two hours."

We still haven't got the picture. More than ever, it often feels as if we are living in a kind of end times. As one who has worked with youth over a lifetime, I can sense a change in this 21st century. No longer do I find the self-satisfied confidence in the future that shone in the youth of the 1970s and 80s. They had a kind of tunnel vision, as if what they were growing up in was going to last forever.

Today, there is a kind of shift in the eyes of youth. I sense an uneasiness on the part of these youth, almost as if asking, "What about the future?" The confidence that used to be there is gone, no more blind optimism. Almost as if they are waiting to strike the iceberg!

Of course, that event, striking the iceberg, is inevitable apart from a turning toward our Lord and Redeemer, Jesus Christ. The turn has to be that specific, not just toward some generic god, but to our Lord Jesus Christ who alone is the way, the truth and the life, through whom we are brought before God our Father. In addition, a half-hearted, mouthed commitment isn't going to make it either. It has to be total and complete, hearts completely opened, minds clearly thinking, hands prepared to work in the name of Christ.

This is a place that the world has never been before. Always in the past, such feelings were limited in scope, in locality, to just a portion of the known world. I believe that is no longer the case. This choice between the empty container of secularism and the chalice of the Blood of Christ has never been more dramatic, never more universal, never more breathtaking.

On top of that, never have we been less prepared for that moment. We live encased in denial, blissfully assuming that no universal event equivalent to the Titanic striking the iceberg could possibly happen today.

5. Cascading Dominoes

> For you have died, and your life is hidden with Christ in God. When Christ your life appears, then you too will appear with him in glory. Put to death, then, the parts of you that are earthly... Because of these the wrath of God is coming. By these you too once conducted yourselves, when you lived in that way.
> Colossians 3:2-5

How unexpected it was that the empty container of secularism outpaced the chalice of the Blood of Christ in our culture. Fifty, sixty, or seventy years is a brief time for such a change to have taken place. Until we look back and reflect on what has happened, we are left surprised, bewildered and confused, both about what has happened to our Catholicism, as well as the suddenness of cultural upheaval in our midst.

It seemed such a small thing, when it happened! The small thing of the 1960s was simply that there was a pill you could now take to prevent a pregnancy from happening, and that would allow for sexual intercourse to occur with supposedly no consequences. Such a small thing: a birth control pill!

Actually, the pill was not the issue. Rather it was the stunning disconnect between the sexual act and the very essence of procreation that the pill highlighted. That primary and fundamental purpose of all humanity toward the begetting of a child, the conception of life was simply cut adrift into a climate of absolute permissiveness. In the end, there is no form of sexual expression that would not be allowed, once the conception of a child is out of the picture.

The bizarre gift of the 1960s and beyond is what we now are facing in the 21st century, a kind of sexual permissiveness virtually unprecedented from the time of the Roman Empire. Now, not only is virtually every form of sex allowed, there is an equal and unprecedented demand from the LGBTQ community, the Democratic National Party, and the media, that all are to support and own this inverted, alternative universe of Satan. If not, you are to be labeled a bigot. It cannot end but in the persecution and disenfranchisement of anyone who would follow the crystal-clear warnings that have come to us in the Gospel and in the Epistles of Saint Paul, and from the consistent teachings of the Church over two millennia.

It turns out that the cascade of change in sexual practice was like dominoes, standing on end, lined up one after another, and the first one tipped against the second, and then the second against the third, and so on, one after another. Well, such was the case with this separation of sexual intercourse from the procreative nature of intercourse. Today, the end is still not in sight. The first domino was that birth control pill, coupled with the disconnect of procreation from the act of sex.

No one, with one exception, grasped the significance of that moment, or that there would be such a chain of fallen dominoes that would continue right into the 21st century. Let's try to characterize a little of what happened.

From the 1960s

First of all, there was the occurrence of what was not supposed to happen now that we had the pill, namely, no more unwanted, unexpected pregnancies. The fact was that any form of birth control was never one hundred percent effective. Sometimes the pills just didn't work, and pregnancies happened.

It was thus another small step from the prevention of a pregnancy to the elimination of a surprise pregnancy, one that wasn't supposed to happen. The world of abortion thus ballooned into a world of pregnancy prevention. That pill, it turned out, was anything but one hundred percent effective. There were errors on the part of remembering to take the pill, and then the way the human body works, and that no medicine always works.

Hence, pregnancy was even more surprising than before. "This wasn't supposed to happen, not anymore; after all I took the pill," or, "She promised to take it!" Thus abortion was redefined, now as an emergency form of pregnancy prevention, no longer "just" the murder of an unborn child.

Thus, with birth control now becoming ubiquitous, a heterosexual climate of permissiveness naturally resulted. In fact, that climate has exploded. Sex without or before marriage, sexual activity between a number of partners — all became possible and desirable. You could experiment; you could hook up. You could have your pleasure, without the burdens of marriage, or the pregnancy that would lead to marriage!

Thus sexual intercourse became a rite of liberation, no longer an act of commitment, no longer an act of impulse, instead it became something that everyone had a right to, anytime, anyway. Sex this way became an entitlement of our culture. It was a major step of postmodern liberation.

Thus, too, did marriage change. Marriage fidelity was weakened, with the vows no longer being something permanent. Divorce multiplied, leaving children in those families without models of fidelity when they themselves would choose a spouse. Parenting has become more and more a lost art.

Eventually there was a perception that even marriage itself was no longer necessary, possibly even an obstacle to one's liberty. On top of that, given that marriage places woman at the heart of marriage and family, the importance of woman shifted downward. Woman is no longer the focus of marriage and family. What has happened to men in this new environment yet remains to be documented. I believe it was nothing good for either man or woman. Both lost dignity and respect, with roles and identity ripped apart in the soup of sexual freedoms.

One has to wonder if this climate that evolved from the 60s might not be a factor in the sexual abuse by clergy. It seemed that all the boundaries that priests were to live by had simply been removed. It was as if all the fences were gone, because nobody remembered that they were there for a purpose. There was a new spirit of permissiveness, a kind of non-accountability that leaked into the lives of priests from the 60s on.

Perhaps it was the result of the boundaries that had disappeared, of the loss of inherent precautions that had been a part of priestly life for a long time, resulting in a kind of numbing confusion for which there is no explanation or accountability.

The Future of Children

Also, there was a subtle consequence of birth control and abortion that disconnected children from marriage, making children unnecessary to whatever a couple chooses to do within their marriage. The consequences of this disconnect has been immense for the future of our culture. Curious how so often couples no longer consider children an intrinsic part of their marriages!

One of the illusions beginning in these last decades was that the world was overpopulated, and that everyone had to stop bringing children into the world. That illusion was so successful that culture after culture around the world is now facing under population among the younger generations, and an over population ballooning among the older ones. In addition, the magic number of children per family dropped significantly in the minds of Catholics.

One wonders if it was not a preoccupation on the part of Catholics about the costs of raising children, but rather the price of individual freedom, and what that would do to the wealth and comfort of the couple. That God's help would be given to the family was often forgotten!

The Catholic Response

Catholicism was caught off guard by these events, by this cascade of dominoes, for which we were unprepared. First of all, *Humanae Vitae*, the encyclical of Blessed Pope Paul VI, rejected artificial birth control. When it came out it was widely opposed, and was followed by an uproar on the part of many in the Church. Priests had a really hard time with it and ran for cover when the encyclical was released. The thinking was that such a stand was going to be too difficult for the average Catholic to support. Besides, the emergence of the pill was such a little thing, with no supposed consequences!

In many ways the consequence was a seismic shift in the Church. The laity went ahead and made their own decisions, thinking, "What harm could the pill do in the long run?" Nobody saw the consequences, that it was the nose of the camel under the tent.

Catholics, then, and especially clergy, naively, were like someone standing on the beach, watching the beginning of a tsunami, wondering what that wave could possibly mean, being so big, not realizing that it was coming for them.

One of the surprising practical results was that many Catholics simply stopped going to confession. Deep down they knew that what they were doing wasn't in line with where our Church was, despite the silence of their priests. Statistically, vast numbers of Catholics chose artificial birth control over against *Humanae Vitae*.

Since that time, for those who still go to confession, seldom has the sin of artificial birth control been confessed. As a part of this lacuna of confession, the entire nature of sin was redefined, excused, and obliterated from the consciences of many. Not only was birth control gone, but sin itself could now be sidestepped and misplaced as well. It was all a kind of indirect side effect to that initial decision about birth control. It was that first domino, now become the tsunami.

Even today, occasionally parents, bringing a child for first confession, have ended up going back to confession with their children, after many years of neglect of that sacrament. Absent from confession for those years, they now seemed not able to recall what sins might have happened over the past fifteen to twenty years. Their consciences had become numbed, anesthetized by the choices they had made and the practices they had adopted in their lives. They forgot how to go to confession and could recall hardly any sins about their younger lives. There was a kind of amnesia for the average Catholic about anything connected to these matters that had transpired since the 1960s. Honestly, they had compromised, adjusted more to the secularism of our times than to the truth of their faith.

The Clergy's Response

The clergy scarcely knew what to do either. To give a homily opposed to artificial birth control would alienate large portions of Catholics. Some tried, but most kept silent. People had made their choice, and didn't want to hear about it.

The parish priest found it difficult to find ways to speak about chastity and purity from the pulpit. Knowing what the liberated Catholics had already decided, the priest often chose silence, rather than to speak up. There was little or no encouragement to seek out the virtues of purity or chastity. In the end, the silence of clergy resulted in a kind of tacit approval of all these new behaviors, a loss all the way around, devastating to the Church as a whole and especially among its youth. The dominoes continued to fall, from generation to generation.

This silence about purity and chastity has resulted in an elephant in the living room that few yet have clearly acknowledged. We have talked about everything but chastity and purity, wondered why the young have lost their way regarding faith, wondering whatever happened to their faith. We have left this matter to fester in silence, not knowing how or whether to approach the topic. Sexual permissiveness is now generally assumed.

When the Son of Man returns, will He find any faith?

Clearly, the dominoes have continued to fall well into the 21st century. Once the permissiveness for heterosexuals and the silence about purity and chastity had spread across the culture, why would not the homosexuals think that they should have equivalent rights on the same basis, as well as an equivalent recognition by the culture. If sex outside of marriage is acceptable behavior, no longer a sin, not needing to be confessed, what's the difference if it's between any two consenting individuals regardless of whom it might be with. If purity and chastity are gone from heterosexuals in this culture, are there any limits left? Just as the battle was lost against the sins of heterosexuality in the 1960s for the Church, so too the battle against the sins of homosexuality were lost by the 2000s.

Thus has come same-sex marriage, and all of the massive changes regarding these matters. In a sense, same-sex marriage, and the breakdown of any limits in these matters is the logical consequence of the choices in our culture—and in some sense, our failure of religion—that have long been growing since the 1960s. It's all in the dominoes. Nor is it a major change of direction on the part of many toward a redefinition of gender, with youth encouraged to make a choice about gender, as if sexuality were irrelevant. This redefinition of gender too is a consequence of the choices and behaviors of the past decades. In a climate of total freedom and entitlement, nothing is prevented, everything is allowed, a kind of hollow victory for secularism, articulated in the supposed absence of the risen Christ.

The Dominoes of the Holy Spirit

There needs to be an immense sadness within the Church about what has transpired. No one anticipated the shattering collapse that has occurred. Within the priesthood, we have not yet come to grips with our own halting and insufficient response to this collapse. Those of us ordained in that era were often mute, speechless about what we were witnessing.

I believe that this cascade of dominoes has even undermined the call of celibacy that God gives to young people to come follow Him, and has resulted in the drop of vocations. The more secularism dominates our youth, the less the call to the priesthood or religious life can be heard.

We have not yet completely found our voices in these matters! At least now, we can see the source of what has happened, and can recognize that we need to clearly and forcefully respond in some way to this secularism. We now know that any response to these matters can't begin with the issue of sexuality, but that this is a consequence of something that precedes that issue, something at the very root of our faith.

The Heart of the Matter, the First New Domino

It seems we need to create our own cascade of dominoes, different ones from those of secularism, in order to respond to this present time, to address this inverted, alternative universe of Satan.

The question is then: What is the first of our own dominoes?

The heart of the matter is to yield our body, mind, and soul to Christ. Only in total conversion to Christ, in giving ourselves over with an absolute trust in Jesus Christ will we have either the strength or the grace to live out our human lives such as the Gospel calls us to. No fudging of our commitment, no partial or incomplete commitment will be enough. Only a total, unbending gift of self to our risen Savior! For us, as Catholics, this conversion of our hearts to Christ is our first domino. This absolute decision would lead us to a renewed sense of chastity and purity, lifting us above any of the destructive currents of the secular world we live within.

Humanae Vitae did address this primary issue in this manner, but no one was listening at that time. Saint Pope John Paul, in his *Theology of the Body*, joined with Blessed Pope Paul in emphasizing that we need to reach the core of our faith in order to recognize what purity and chastity are about. Saint Pope John Paul is explicit in saying that only in relation to Christ can we know the identity that God has in store for us, right down to our sexuality, that we cannot define exactly what our sexuality might be until we have addressed from where our creation has arisen, and how the cross has transformed how we see our lives in this world.

In *Humanae Vitae* Blessed Pope Paul VI addressed what has been the teaching of the faith from the earliest days, that our sexuality in Christ is part of what identifies who we are, and that our living the faith life is intrinsic to our sexuality. That calling demands that only in Christ are we capable of grasping the meaning of the way to live here in the 21st century.

This means lives given over completely to Christ, as we have never done before, no half measures, no compromises, rather a complete and total yielding to the presence of Christ in our midst. This decision can best be centered and reinforced in the celebration of the Eucharist, in the opening of our hearts to the Sacrament of Penance, in learning patience and selflessness, and living with a sense of purity and chastity as best as we can muster.

Marriage for us who are Catholic needs to be lifelong, a once in a lifetime commitment made clearly and consciously, unbreakable and sacrificial, made in the presence of Christ, all the while remaining pure and chaste within the bounds of marriage. The celibate priest, religious, or monk need to see their life as a total commitment also to the same kind of purity and chastity, different, of course, from that of marriage.

Purity and Chastity for Our Times

It is not unusual in this culture of permissiveness, that a Catholic might awaken to how distorted their life might have become with regard to purity and chastity. Part of what we need to understand is that there is a way back, a way to return and become a new person in Christ, even after having gone the way of secularism. This is an issue of prayer and sacrificial dedication for the Church in the 21st century. People caught in this mess of a world need to know that there is a way home, that Christ awaits at the door for them, that there is hope for a renewed life in Christ. The sexual morass of these times is not an abyss from which the sincerely repentant cannot find escape. We never lose hope for those around us, that have left us. Most in this world are equivalent to victims of this evil, of a kind seldom seen in past history.

My concern is that we might give up on our pursuit of chastity and purity ourselves, thinking it to be impossible in these times, given the weaknesses that we have inherited from Adam and Eve. Chastity and purity may seem impossible to many in nowadays. However, what is not impossible is that each of us has the power to turn our lives over to Christ as best we can, knowing that he has the power over the supposedly impossible.

This issue of purity and chastity, once we have centered our lives and our hearts on Christ, can then be addressed with sincerity and hope by every Catholic person and in every marriage. The grace and mercy of Christ in our lives alone is strong enough to saturate our souls and minds for the challenge of our times. Courage and determination, coupled with the grace and mercy of

Christ, will bring us closer day by day to the purity and chastity that the Gospel and the Scriptures teach us.

Our Contemporary Challenge

We must believe that it is possible, in Christ, to live in a new and deeper way, in this holy way, with total respect for the opposite sex, for children, for marriage, and for celibacy. In short, purity and chastity must be seen as both possible and deeply precious, especially in this postmodern era. As Saint Paul says,

> That you may be blameless and innocent,
> children of God without blemish in the midst
> of a crooked and perverse generation, among
> whom you shine like lights in the world.
> (Philippians 2:15)

This was precisely the gift of the Gospel to the first days of the early Church, as it spread throughout Europe and Asia, opening the minds of the converts to a sacred sense of sex, that defined itself in terms only of marriage or celibacy, totally different from the sexual practices of the Roman Empire. Their fundamental discovery was that there was a pathway to living that did not require the abandonment of what was deepest and purest in their nature about their sexuality.

This new way, this new creation taught generations that sex was sacred and could be redirected properly to both marriage and celibacy, resulting in a clarity that purity and chastity were both possible and worth seeking. This knowledge changed the first Christians to a deep and never before recognized sense of worth in their lives. It clearly stunned the minds and hearts of those who had been converted to Christianity, just as it shocked the Roman Empire.

This same awareness is precisely what will be required today of those who are Catholic, and wish to give themselves totally to God's plan of salvation. Only when we understand the cascade of dominoes that began in the 1960s, and that continues even today, deeper and deeper into an empty secular way of living, into the alternative, inverted universe of Satan—only then will we have the courage and determination to live completely in the way of Jesus Christ, with purity and chastity progressing into the heart of our lives.

I am certain also that the only completely reliable pathway to attain such a union with Christ will have to be our complete attentiveness to the core of the Mass, that our lives must center themselves precisely on the moment of Christ's sacrificial giving of Himself to the Father, in exchange for our redemption. We must maintain an appreciation of what is deepest in the Eucharist in order to live in the vapid wasteland of secularism that surrounds us today.

The Pathway to the Future for Us

I think it crucial for us to understand what has happened over the past fifty, sixty, or seventy years. While we often didn't understand where all of this atmosphere of secularism came from before, now we can realize what it is that we will have to do, to face up to what it is that surrounds us.

1. We will have to deepen our commitment to Christ, in a way that never seemed necessary before. In this, prayer is at the core!
2. We have to make a dedicated effort toward purity

and chastity in our lives in a way never focused on before.
3. We will have to understand the centrality of the Mass in our spiritual lives in a new and deepened way.
4. Also we must utilize the Sacrament of Confession in a deeper way, in order to walk with Christ in this way that has been so abandoned in our times.

There are, of course, more steps than these, but these first steps are a strong beginning that will sustain our faith in such an empty and meaningless (as well as evil) environment. We need to understand what secularism's chaos is sowing in our era. We must find our own dominoes, and let them fall one after another into a deeper schema of Faith. We must recognize the dominoes of secularism well enough to recognize the difference from our own.

In the end, our own set of dominoes will open our hearts to whatever the call that lies before us might be, whether it be a better openness to our marriages, a new openness to the number of children, or a call to the celibate life in the priesthood or the vowed life. In all of this, if we get the first spiritual dominoes in line, that Jesus Christ is the exact center of our lives, then, the Holy Spirit will lead us to the renewal of the hearts and minds of our culture.

6. The Secret We Have: The Risen Christ

> Moses was tending the flock of his father-in-law Jethro, the priest of Midian. Leading the flock beyond the wilderness, he came to the mountain of God, Horeb. There the angel of the Lord appeared to him as fire flaming out of a bush. When he looked, although the bush was on fire, it was not being consumed. So Moses decided, "I must turn aside to look at this remarkable sight. Why does the bush not burn up?"
> Exodus 3:1-3

Recently in a park nearby, I witnessed three teens or young adults walking together. The curious thing was that each of them was holding a cell phone, each staring intently into their phone.

Surrounding them was a view of nature, a mixture of pine and oak trees, reaching to the blue sky above. The forest was a rich green carpet under a dense canopy of leaf and underbrush. The wind and the silence was almost theological.

None of the three was looking at what surrounded them, nor were they looking at each other. I could imagine that the three of them might have been close in friendship, what might have been a spirit of togetherness saturated with the abundance of nature. Instead, their eyes and thoughts were lost in their cell phones, inattentive to each other.

What an apt symbol for our times. Had the cell phone been invented and common for the two on the road to Emmaus, they would have missed the presence of the risen Christ with them, not having heard the words of Christ reinterpreting for them the experience of the last several days, not recognizing him in the breaking of the bread.

Recognizing the Suppression of Christ's Presence Today

One wonders if the cell phone might just be a symbol of the block that keeps our contemporary world from recognizing the risen Christ in our midst. Could it be that the solipsism like that of the cell phone is part of what isolates us from the presence of Christ in the Eucharist.

That's pushing it, probably, for the sake of an analogy. Nonetheless something about our world today prevents a recognition of the risen Christ in our midst. Our postmodern world doesn't even have the radar necessary to look for the risen Christ who is here with us.

You can look and look and look for eggs in an auto parts store, or for batteries in a pet store. So too, where do you look to find the risen Christ in today's world, in this culture? Do we even know enough to look for Him? Could our times be that far gone?

The fact is, not only can people not find the risen Christ today, there is the assumption that he never really existed, or never rose from the dead. He is just gone, plain and simple. He is irrelevant for today's world and culture. He is so absent that the only thing left to attack is the Church itself.

Christ Is the Head, We Are the Body

Recently I attended a panel at a college campus with about 15 local Protestant ministers. Each of us shared our stories about our journey of faith, many of which were beautifully told. Following that, there was a question and answer time. One of the questions was: "If Christ were to come today, which church would he join?"

None of us on the panel wanted or even knew where to go with this question in such an ecumenical environment. However, later the question would not go away from me. Of course, the simplest response should have been that Christ is not a member of any church, he is the head. Ephesians and Philippians addresses it directly: Christ is the head, we are the body.

I was once visited by a stranger at my parish. It was the Feast of Our Lady of Guadalupe in our parish, and her shrine was surrounded by hundreds of roses that the Hispanic community had brought during the night. The fragrance of the roses wafted over the whole interior of the church.

This stranger appeared to be a young man, perhaps in his thirties, dressed as any worker might be. He came and sat down in the pew in front of me, and we started a conversation. I asked him if he knew Jesus in his heart, and he said that he did. Then I asked another question that seemed to me to be the acid test of the postmodern world, "What did he think of the Church?" With Christ irrelevant to the now secular reality, all that is left to dispatch from our times is this Church that keeps insisting on issues of morality.

I did not expect his answer. He said that I should think of the burning bush that Moses saw, and that would show me the relation of the Church to Christ. He explained that, while the bush itself was dry and lifeless in itself, the fire was alive in its midst. Thus the focus is always to remain on the fire at the center, the risen Christ. I had never thought about it that way. I thought of Moses' observation: "Why does the bush not burn up?"

Then I was distracted by someone for a moment, and when I turned back to this stranger, he was gone. But not about of what he had spoken to me!

In a sense, that image of the burning bush showed the inseparability of Christ and the Church, highlighting especially the dependency of the Church on the fire at its center. The image also brings me to reconsider our times and culture today, as the criticism and judgment of the Church for its morals, for being so out of touch with the times, for seeming to be so backward in the issues of the day.

This image also highlights from where the beauty and truth of the Church arises. When Christ is at the center, all of the richness of the Church is illuminated. We are a reflection of the risen Christ in our midst. Once Christ is at our center, all that the Church teaches, all of the saints in our history, all of the rites and orders, all the roles that exist, slip quietly into place for us.

Christ and Church Divided Today

Fundamental to this unity of Christ with His Church is the choice that each of us has to make about Christ in our hearts, that we must take Him in, that we must yield ourselves to His plan. Once we do that important step, our minds and hearts open up to understanding how the Church is an essential dimension of Jesus Christ. Without that fundamental step, we see the Church only in pieces or fragments. But with Christ, those pieces fall into an organic whole of truths and goodness that make sense in every way.

It seems as if the secular culture wants to split Christ and the Church into separate entities. The motivation for this division lies at the heart of our desires for this world. Skipping the essential step of conversion to Christ, to them the Church becomes incomprehensible and repugnant. "Who is the Church, to tell me what to do?" Now, because Christ has been scrubbed from their consciousness, all that is left is the Church, seemingly a dead, dried bush in the desert, with no fire, easy to dispose of, easy to trash.

Then I refocused the question a bit for myself. Suppose that deep in the heart of our culture, the issue of the risen Christ is still central, but you can't go there anymore and maintain your lifestyle. We know that when you are called by Christ, it's something of a blank check, to go and do what He asks of you, whenever He asks. Our yes is to have no conditions and is often without a vision of where it might lead. The yes comes first, and what Christ will do with that, only He knows.

No wonder we try to run from His presence. No wonder the Church frightens us. We have our own agenda, and it is not that of Christ. So, it is not that Christ is gone, he is just too dangerous to be conceived of. And, the Church is an annoying reminder of that presence. The self-centeredness of the culture is so pervasive that it dares not even consider the Christ who is so central to our lives and existence.

The Ultimate Stumbling Block of the Church

I think that no one can eventually escape looking at the face of Christ at some point in this life. You simply can't erase Christ from the core of our hearts. Perhaps the risen Christ is just too scary today, and so it becomes easier to turn and focus on the Church, than to have to deal with the Christ in our midst. So we'll pretend that Christ is no longer an issue, and then the Church simply looks like just another human institution, a poorly organized one at that, one weak at communications and public relations.

As Christ is suppressed in the consciousness of the modern mind, the Church becomes the stumbling block in its attempt at the denial of the risen Christ for our times and our lives. It's an inverse proportion, the less Christ, the more the Church is the focus. It's easy to reject the Church these days, as long as Christ does not have to be taken into account with it.

How often we have heard of someone who just can't stomach the Church anymore, and has left, but with the question of Christ's presence left unasked. In all the stories we have heard of people "leaving the church," there never seems any mention of also leaving behind Jesus Christ, His presence in the Eucharist, our need that Christ walk with us day by day and moment by moment, or our need for the forgiveness of sins, our need for the grace and mercy that flows through that Church. Are we then to redeem ourselves?

I'm curious. What happens at the end, either at death or at the final coming, when we have to finally meet the risen Lord, and have to stand before him? If we have denied His existence, and defeated the yearning of our hearts for Christ, will we recognize him then? If we evaded Christ in this world, having cast away the body of which Christ is the head, what will we do with Him in the next? Will we even know who He is?

7. Oxygen Level Critical

For I am convinced that neither death, nor life, nor angels, nor principalities, nor present things, nor future things, nor powers, nor height, nor depth, nor any other creature will be able to separate us from the love of God in Christ Jesus our Lord.
Romans 8:38-39

There is almost no oxygen left. In our postmodern world many are left gasping. Almost everything is gone. There is no origin, no destiny, no identity, no purpose in a secular age such as ours. Many have lost soul and self. The common good is gone. In a secular context, who one might be is reduced to a brand, to whatever image can be projected, because there is nothing of substance in identity.

When the Father and the Son, Jesus Christ, are gone, disappeared, removed from the center of things, we are left with nothing but ourselves. We are not designed to be the center of our own lives. We are children of God, and if God is not there, who are we but lost children, hopelessly careening around in search of whoever we might be. We thus become floating fragments in an alphabet soup of total freedom. And, in the postmodern world, God is indeed gone! If God is dead, so are we. No wonder the popularity of the walking dead on television today. No wonder we find the walking dead so frightening; it's us without the Trinity.

The Consequences of No Divine Existence

In addition, then, the trouble is just beginning. There is no redemption, no forgiveness, no salvation whatsoever. Death is a travesty; life is arbitrary. We see fragments of morality and human rights free floating, connected to nothing but to our will and desires. There is no sacrifice, no need for commitment. This is our life, and you only go around once. There is nothing else. The last frontier seems to be sexuality, perhaps opioids, even suicide.

Still worse, there is no redeemer in this secular world. Jesus Christ has been scrubbed from consciousness. After all, he is two thousand years distant! Our Savior has been rendered mute in this world. His presence is not felt, His love unrequited. Search as you will outside of the Church, Christ seems not there, the story of His presence untold. It's all psychology, without Christ, even though that doesn't work. Science just answers the wrong questions. Technology leaves us hanging.

The risen Christ, in this postmodern world, seems an obsolete illusion. His presence cannot even be imagined. Talk of Him is not allowed. He is gone, simply gone from any spark of awareness. Invisible means not there. For us who are disciples of Christ, we can barely breathe in that atmosphere. For that matter, neither can our postmodern world.

Recently I read of someone using a Google Assistant. He asked, "Who is Jesus Christ?" to the assistant. There was no answer. He asked about Satan and the devil, and got a long detailed response. Then he asked about Charles Manson, the murderer some thirty years ago in Los Angeles, and also receive a long, detailed response. I suspect the same responses would come from Siri or

Alexa. For some reason, Jesus Christ is a question that can't be asked or answered today!

Curiously, the existence of demons, vampires, extraterrestrials, the walking dead, witches, and devils are continuously portrayed in the media. Somehow, they're okay. They are a kind of creeping, allowable, backdoor reconstruction of the spiritual today, in bizarre, violent dimensions. Again, it's Satan's inverted, alternative universe.

Even angels might be acceptable in this strange new world, but not Jesus Christ, risen from the dead, present in our midst! One wonders why, why one form of the invisible and hidden is acceptable, but another, the risen Christ, is not? There are clearly new rules about what can exist and what is not allowed, about what you can see and what you cannot.

Secularism, also Hidden but Afraid

The Church is an easy target in this secular world. It is the last visible element of our spirituality, and it is hated. In this kind of world the Church is connected to nothing. How could it be? If God and Christ are gone, where does the Church fit? Surely it is not the Body of Christ. It's free floating and headless, like modern morality. It has no basis in science. It is an archaic obstruction to what the world wants and to what is coming. It is easily dismissed. The Sacred Scriptures are left unread, and appear incomprehensible in this climate. There is no oxygen here either.

In point of fact, I believe the postmodern world is terrified of the risen Christ. They dare not go there, because of what they might find, and the questions He might ask! Better to leave God dead, to condemn the Church than to deal with Christ risen from the dead, hidden but walking in our midst. The real problem is that He is in fact the judge of the living and the dead. How will we ever account for what we have done in this world, of which He is King? Can we ignore Him for decades, for a century, and then ask for forgiveness?

The trouble is that this new world of the secular is camouflaged for the most part, hidden away just below the surface. The average Catholic may not even be aware that something is missing, that the package of secularism simply doesn't add up, that it is a void, and that there really is no oxygen left in that world view. Last of all, we don't realize that this model of life and existence is toxic to all that is about faith, a form of acid that eats away marriages, families, and the young who are coasting along, unintentionally drifting in this strange wasteland of secularism.

It appears that only those who aggressively hold on to the faith that they possess will survive this nihilism, the nothingness of the postmodern lifestyle, this absence of oxygen.

This is the point where we need to begin to address the importance of the Mass and Eucharist in our lives. There is oxygen here in the Mass! Spiritually, the best oxygen can be found in the Eucharist. The need for awareness here is massive. To be Catholic in this era literally demands something of a warrior's stance, a determined pushback against the inertia of this new world. Everything outside of the Mass and Eucharist comes up short today in this vapid atmosphere.

It appears that we have tried everything else in our times to deal with this emptiness foisted upon our lives. We have tried very hard at everything else, to no avail.

Time and again, I have offered to begin programs in the parish and the programs died because Catholics had no time available to meet weekly or more than weekly, or even on Sundays, about their faith and prayer. Then,

I would drive by Little League baseball fields or soccer fields where the parking lots would be filled on a Tuesday evening. That same Tuesday evening, the church parking lot is empty.

There was plenty of time for that kind of social activity, none for Christ and faith. Weekend after weekend, there were traveling teams for youth hockey, volleyball, and soccer, where weeks go by without seeing the family in church. They were always away for the weekend for their children. Plenty of time there! Holy Week, we're gone on spring break!

For fifty years, from generation to generation, I have watched the growth of this decay in the lives of Catholics, choosing compromise rather than dedication to the faith. Our list of priorities seems to have no place for Christ or for the love that can only come from the Father of all.

The Antidote to Secularism

There is only one antidote that I can see for Catholics over all this time. That antidote starts with the Mass, the Eucharist. Only with the awareness of the risen Christ in our midst, that flows from the Eucharist, can we stem the flow of desertion from the faith into this new world of secular lifestyles. Only by taking Christ into our hearts in the Eucharist can we hope to have the inner strength that is necessary to resist such nihilism. Only by owning a faith nourished by the Eucharist that is the backbone of our daily lives can we hope to sustain our faith in Christ. Here alone there is oxygen!

What is necessary today is a deep and personal relationship with the risen Christ, with hearts turned directly toward Him, recognizing Him with the eyes of faith, sensing His voice in the pages of the Sacred

Scriptures. It is absolutely essential today that we take Him into our hearts on a regular basis. And nothing is better at this than the Mass and the Eucharist.

Witness our times as the absence of Christ's presence. Why is it that we don't see the climate change going on before our eyes? Why is it that alcohol and opioids ruin so many lives and families? What possible outcome can arise from identity politics? Whatever happened to marriage? What is the next step in the unravelling of our culture? So, how is it going for our world today, trying to live on its own, as if there were no God, no risen Christ?

It is said that chocolate is the answer. If chocolate is not, the question is wrong. Similarly, in reality every issue leads to the risen Christ in our midst. He is the answer. And that answer starts with the Mass.

Part II

The Mass We Celebrate

8. The Spiritual Dimension of the Mass

> At that time people will say to the mountains,
> "Fall upon us!" and to the hills, "Cover us!" for
> if these things are done when the wood is green
> what will happen when it is dry?
> Luke 23:30-31

We stand at the threshold of alarming changes. The culture sidles along aimlessly, deeper into a period of godlessness, a kind of functional if not intentional agnosticism. Somehow over the past decades, we have witnessed a cascade of dominoes, the breakup of many of the values and virtues that we hold dear. We now know where this came from, when humanity forgot that they had come from above, from God. For all centuries earlier, we knew where we came from, even when we rebelled against Him. There was a kind of chain of being that started with God beyond it all, then the angels, then us, next the animals, and finally inanimate objects.

While he didn't originate the change, Descartes gave us the point of redefinition: "I think, therefore I am." With that simple statement, he unwittingly redefined everything. Humanity was now the center, not God. In addition, if humanity was at the center of things, no longer was grace necessary, only nature was needed. We could be self-sufficient, and didn't need God's help. In fact, it became apparent that God was no longer above and beyond that chain. We were, all by ourselves, with nothing above us. Likewise, once we were at the center, original sin disappeared from consciousness. Without that awareness of the Fall, now our modern world could begin to think that everything was within their grasp. In the end, "We are now gods."

Probably nobody understood the consequences of that kind of thinking, but clearly there was a four hundred year cascade of change that has brought us to where we are today.

Another consequence was morality. As Dostoyevsky said, "If God is dead, all is permitted." Once that break from God was chosen, that decision made, that denial articulated, coupled with the wealth and technology of the present times, this postmodern world was born. Generation to generation, the drift is further and further away from the Christianity of the past. Humanity can now be and intends to be anything it wants to be, no boundaries, whatever power allows, awash in freedom, drowning in it, in fact.

Past the Threshold, No Room for Compromise

We are now beyond the point where politics might alter the outcome, or where protest might influence the direction our world is drifting. Furthermore, thinking we can engage the contemporary times in a dialogue, as if we can appeal to their better selves, is simply illusion, or even worse, appeasement. This world knows where it is going, and clearly chooses to go there.

The poles couldn't be any more opposed and distant from each other: the godlessness of the times versus the presence of Christ and the Father with us in the Eucharist. It is the Blood of the Chalice versus the empty container of our age, a forced choice, no room for compromise, no middle ground.

We couldn't be any further apart than these two issues. One is about absence and non-existence, the other is about presence, the presence of the risen Christ offering Himself to the Father for all of humanity. One is about an emptiness of a creator-less world, the other about the most sacred moment in the history of the created world. One is about being alone in a universe with no eternity, no content, the other about a hope rich with meaning, saturated with the love of God.

The Mass in the Postmodern World

Nothing in our quiver of arrows regarding these times is as important as the Mass. This is because the Mass is the deepest touchstone of the presence of Christ in our hearts. If this were not true about the Mass, then Jesus Christ would have instituted something else at the Last Supper. In the same way, as recorded in John 6, Jesus would not have said four times in different ways that "Unless you eat my body and drink my blood...."

The Word of God is important, as is prayer. We desperately need Adoration. The Sacraments help to sustain us, but it is the Mass that is the heart and soul of our Catholicism, the beacon of light shining on our times. Nothing is more powerful and more relevant to these times than the Mass. Nothing takes us to the pinnacle of truth and depth of divine love as does the Mass. The Mass holds us in the moment of the climax of all history.

Thus it is critical that we understand the central moment of the Mass with a depth and scope as never before. The Mass cannot be routine, and we cannot be passive in its celebration. The Mass needs to be intense and personal, with a keen awareness of the presence of the risen Christ with us. Nothing short of the Mass will fortify us for the days ahead.

When we think like this world thinks, we could easily end up believing that the Mass would be the worst possible antidote to these times. After all, the Mass is not much of a wedge and has no leverage against the direction that our world is taking. The Mass has a certain kind of powerlessness. How could it be that something as indirect and hidden as the Mass could be the instrument of such power, as spiritual as it is, over against everything that the world of today is, with all its manipulation of the media, its control of public education, its unbridled selfishness?

My thesis is this: only the spiritual dimensions of the Mass will fortify in us the strength to address what our world is today. Nothing will illuminate these times like the mystery of the cross that we celebrate in the Eucharist. In the Mass we arrive at the deepest contact we can have with Christ, risen but hidden, allowing us to live in Christ, becoming more and more one with Him in all that we do. Only Christ and the Spirit can interpret for us how to deal with these times in which we live.

The Mass can be our antidote. Only in Christ will it be possible to address these postmodern times. Nothing beyond the Mass gets closer to the essential moment of the cross, to the moment of self-giving and sacrifice by Christ and to the simultaneous moment of the Father's acceptance of Christ's gift on our behalf.

The Will, that Drives Everything Today

Let's be specific about where and when we are living, about what is challenging the heart and soul of the 21st century. The central change in our American culture has been the growing sense of entitlement that we Americans have, that we should be free to choose whatever will meet our own needs and wants. This sense arises from the lack of a connection to the risen Christ and to His Father. We end up saying, "It's my right to live my own life, without interference." This way of life makes everyone lord and ruler of their own lives, without interference from anyone else. Our will is our sovereign, and it's totally individualistic.

In this culture we have become, in a sense, gods, able to define ourselves, satisfy our desires, and live untrammeled lives in total freedom. We are generally willfully ignorant of the common good, isolated from any politics other than what will satisfy us. We see ourselves as ranking ahead of the rest of humanity. We have lost history, civics, and morality, one after another. All should stay out of my way, my life, my happiness. I have no obligations, no responsibility, no duty except to live my very own life without interference.

I believe all of these traits stem clearly from willful amnesia about the risen Christ, to whom we are to be subjects and disciples. God the Father counts as a loss in our world today, gone missing.

In the midst of that context, the 21st century appears to be pointing us down a new road, one that includes the massive changes in climate, artificial intelligence, and the continuing distortion of wealth between the rich and the poor. For the present, few are paying attention, most just going their own way.

What if the future will demand sacrifice and selflessness in order for our culture to survive? What if we are lost in our entitlement, and the future begins to look catastrophic in makeup? Sacrifice and selflessness can only come from above, with our committed discipleship in Jesus Christ.

My point is not to enumerate these potential harms of the future that could mean the collapse of our era. The only response to the danger of collapse of our culture that could come is to find a spiritual connection again at the heart of our faith. The incipient agnosticism of the postmodern world, manifested in the entitlements we think we have, cannot provide us with the energy and insight to navigate the times that we are in.

If it's like this in the green wood, what will it be in the dry? Where can we turn to find the discipline, the heart, the commitment to address such a time? Where can we go to learn the ability of self-sacrifice and selflessness that will be necessary for the days ahead? We are living in a land of endless entitlement, in an era of unlimited freedom. If examined closely, that kind of freedom is just another word for total slavery.

The Choice Before Us

The Sacrifice of the Mass can reorient ourselves. The Mass is gyroscopic, orienting us to think and act clearly in spiritual ways, keeping us upright and on balance. The Mass is the one mystery that gets to the heart of the matter, that gives us the backbone to hold fast to who and what we are in the midst of shattering changes. The Eucharist calls us to look deeply inward, into the source of faith and truth that can only come from the presence and love of the risen Lord, from the mystery of the Cross, and from the mysterious love of the Father in heaven for us.

I believe that it is time for us to move beyond the problems that appear so huge, beyond the spiraling, downward drift of all that we have tried to hold back from. Instead, we as Catholics have to move on to what it is that will sustain us, and to what we will be able to contribute to the future of our culture. I believe that we can best do that by first centering ourselves, by focusing ourselves in the mystery of the Eucharist, around the presence of Christ with us. The Mass is the starting point for the future of Catholicism in our times, not superficially, but fervently and decisively, with a firm grip on the central moment of all of history that the cross, revealed carefully in the Mass, is for us now.

9. A Diamond in a Bed of Gravel

Yet I live, no longer I, but Christ lives in me; insofar as I now live in the flesh, I live by faith in the Son of God who has loved me and given himself up for me.
Galatians 2:20

I once heard a story about Frank Lloyd Wright, the famous American architect. He had designed a building that sat on a single, central pillar, with no other support but that pillar. Because it was located perfectly in the center of the building, evenly balanced all the way around, the single pillar was enough for support. However, the building still looked somewhat unstable, seeming almost as if it were floating in midair. Because the pillar was perfectly centered, the building was safe.

The building inspectors came along, and having seen nothing like that before, refused to award the construction any approval for use. Wright apparently demonstrated with another simple piece that a perfectly balanced central pillar could sustain a much greater amount of weight than what he had constructed in his architecture. However it was just too much for the inspectors who wouldn't believe or approve of such construction. They couldn't believe that a building could have such a foundation of support, that something could be supported by a single, central pillar.

Our Central Pillar

We have an analogous situation with regard to our faith in this generation. The central pillar, of course, is the risen Christ. We are so used to seeing elaborate art and illustrations of all the parts of the Church that surround the faith community, we find it difficult to believe that Christ Himself might be enough to sustain us in our faith.

Perhaps it is because we are singularly blessed with many aspects of the Church, that we come to believe that the central pillar for us is the Church itself, and we simply take Christ for granted at the center. At times, I wonder if it has been as if we thought that if we surrounded ourselves with enough sacred imagery, enough religious statues, enough religious music, we could take the presence of Christ for granted. All that is a help, but today if you lack an awareness of the love of Christ and His Father for you personally, at dead center, all that stuff around us is not enough anymore. Christianity in the end rises and falls with that central pillar.

As an illustration, in my younger days I was charged with the challenge of starting a parish. I was also to build a school with the church. The location was in a rapidly developing neighborhood, with young couples residing there, most of whom had at least young children, were deep in debt for their education loans, and had just made the purchase of a new home. As a new parish, there was no money floating around loose anywhere, and at that time, as yet, there were not even any parishioners registered in this parish that just had been established.

However, within four years we had put up a shell of a church, along with seven classrooms. We opened the school with one section each of kindergarten through third grade, and immediately started construction on another seven classrooms, then a gym, and finally seven more classrooms, after rolling up a debt of about three million. After those first four years we had only 230 households, but over a period of 12 years we had grown to about 900 families.

The church building is what interests me here. It was a shell, a totally white building, with diamond windows at the east and west ends, with three dormer windows in the north and south ends. From the outside, it looked almost as if it were a house. The inside was unfinished, also white. The windows were clear glass, the floor cement, with no statues or art. Four pillars held up the steeply inclined ceiling. As a shell it was beautiful in itself, but it surely lacked the decorations of the usual American Catholic Church. At the time, it was all we could afford, the school being the first priority.

All we had was an altar, an ambo (lectern), and a baptistry. There was a processional cross. The inside of the church was virtually bare, not by intent, but because of the cost of the school portion.

One might think that this could not possibly meet the needs of a parish community, living in such stark simplicity. However we had one thing, one thing only, and that was that we felt the presence of the risen Christ in our midst, in liturgy after liturgy. The absence of anything else meant we had to focus on the risen Christ in our midst, and on the Spirit that He sent to us. Throughout all that time of construction and debt, we had the central pillar of the parish, Christ Himself with us, in the Mass and the Eucharist. His presence informed our school, our children, our homes and families.

There were those who came that thought something was missing. One time, I had visited a Catholic church in the Back Bay of Boston that left me very jealous. There were statues of saints galore, wonderful stations of the cross, magnificent stained-glass windows, all of it at a level that a contemporary Catholic church could never duplicate, starting from scratch. It had been constructed in the 1880s.

Yet what this new parish had was life giving and sustaining for these young families. The new parish radiated with the presence of the Spirit.

The Absolute Center

There is a lesson here, that in this age of secularism what is required first is a complete and thorough grasp of the central piece of our Catholicism. That center is Christ Himself, who must absolutely be deeply held in our hearts, never wavering in our ownership of who it is that is the center of our lives, our families, our marriages, and our hearts.

The peripherals won't hold today. We can't coast through our Catholic lives, expecting what surrounds us to hold us together, to keep us safe and connected to the Mass and the Eucharist. The fact is, that we are either deeply committed to Christ in our faith, or we simply will lose it in the wandering agnosticism of the 21st century, or in the virulent secularism that seeks to destroy Catholicism. We absolutely have to know Christ in a way that previous generation perhaps did not, and we, each of us as a person, have to know him in depth. In the past, there have always been those who did live this way with Christ. The difference now is that more of us, virtually all of us, the entire parish community, must live this way. There is no margin of failure today.

There have always been saints within the Church in every age, but many others could hold on to their faith in the margins, one foot in and one out. No more. What we need today are more saints, more followers of Christ who are deeply committed to His love, more who are fully immersed in the truth of the Gospels, more that are willing to die for Christ. In the end, this knowledge of Christ in our lives will require an attention to detail, sacramentally and in prayer, living our faith 24/7.

The wealth and technology, the availability of the goods of this world, the media and marketplace are such that we are inundated from childhood by a completely secular world. We easily lose our way in this world, from which earlier generations were somewhat protected.

In this secular context we become convinced that we can do it by ourselves, and then, we are in trouble. When this starts to happen, we are caught off guard. We don't realize that if you don't intentionally choose to make Christ the center of your life, the secular world automatically becomes that center. Sadly we often don't recognize what is happening to us. We lose our way easily, and don't even realize that we are losing it inch by inch.

Our Hidden Resource

The primary way this centrality of Christ in our midst can be held is to understand completely what it is that brings us together in the Mass. This is our hidden but fundamental resource. We have to dig down deeply into the meaning and central moment of Christ giving up His body and pouring out his blood. We must draw near to the hidden mysteries in every celebration of the Eucharist.

We absolutely have to recognize the overarching love of the Father for each of us that is at the climax of the Eucharistic prayer, that what He did for us in sending His Son to die on the cross has exceeded any and all other forms of love that could have been manifested. We have to take our Communion in utter seriousness, knowing exactly what is happening when we receive the

Body and Blood of Christ. We need to become absolutely one with Christ, both ritually and in fact.

All these things have to be clear in our minds, because of the temptations today. Logistically, Satan could not have arrived at a better plan than to indoctrinate our lives from start to finish as if there were no God, no Christ, that the mystery of the Eucharist is none other than myth, that the Church is an obstacle to our human fulfillment, and that we have the right, the entitlement to take anything we want in this world without consequence. The 21st century is the fork in the road of faith. It is either Christ, or it is a creeping nothingness that anesthetizes us.

The Mass in today's world is in a unique situation. The world around us seems to have been reduced to only what science can verify through measurable methods. Nothing else seems to exist except that. Yet, here is the Mass of the Catholic Church, an action laced through with mystery, centered on the invisible presence of Jesus Christ, camouflaged under the form of bread and wine, none of which is verifiable or fact in the minds of much of the culture outside of the Catholic Church.

The Diamond that We Have

To our mind, when fully Catholic, the Mass stands out in this age like a diamond in a bed of gravel, an instrument of beauty and richness, a manifestation of goodness and holiness over against the nothingness and emptiness of a culture gone awry, one unable to find its source of life, its purpose in being here, or where it's going. It is silence over against dissonance, mystery over against the measurable, a diamond in a bed of gravel. The Mass is the road sign of revealed truth.

The culture remains a cacophony of conflict and chaos, pointing in no particular direction, allowing everything, full of itself, unhinged in its morality. The unintended consequences of living without God the Father in heaven are now in full flower. Jesus Christ is a distant memory to this world today, as if He were a man who never was, and the Scriptures, just a quaint old book. No wonder that the Mass seems so out of sync with so much of this culture.

A person walks into a Catholic church for the first time, expecting nothing, but finds himself touched by a presence. Seldom anywhere is there felt such silence. In fact, it is the silence that is so captivating. Nothing seems in motion, everything at rest. A little like Doctor Who's police call box, the Church is bigger on the inside than on the outside, much bigger. There is more space here than is possible to absorb.

Funny how in a Mass sometimes you can be more present to yourself and your life than anywhere else. No wonder some cannot tolerate the atmosphere of a church, especially if they are not at one with themselves or their life. A church is not for everyone it seems. A building like this should not be a place of confrontation, but it is if you are absorbed with the nihilism of these times.

We have arrived at the starting point for Catholicism in the 21st century: it is the awareness of Christ, risen and present with us, and that presence saturates the meaning of the Eucharist and redefines how we are to live in the midst of this strange and empty era.

10. The Dimensions of the Mass

> For when peaceful stillness encompassed everything
> and the night in its swift course was half spent,
> Your all-powerful word from heaven's royal throne
> leapt into the doomed land.
> Wisdom 18:14-15

Clearly our times are difficult from the standpoint of faith. What is offered to us in this culture is only a fragmented and gnarled context, yet it looks so easy and comfortable. As my life has gone on and the years of priesthood are extended, I am amazed at what the Mass has become for me, an absolute contradiction to all that the culture is. I find the Mass a context of silence and beauty that constantly surprises and awes me.

The Mass, the Eucharist, in all its parts has taken on for me a meaning very close to the feelings I have for the Sacred Scriptures, especially the Gospels. I would never tamper with the words of Sacred Scripture or abandon any one of the books of the Bible as being less important than the whole. This is the Word of God, it is inspired!

I now feel a similar way regarding the Mass, finding meaning in each phrase, none of which ought to be tampered with, all of it sacred. Every word counts.

The Church has refined the Mass texts, which were in Latin for centuries, into the language now of English. It has been about a 60-year task, carefully making sure that the words reflect exactly the meaning that they should.

That in itself is awe inspiring. For instance, Why does the consecration use the participles "raised up" and "poured out"? Why is it "the" sign of peace, and not just "a" sign of peace? How is the offering different when the priest says, "my sacrifice" and "yours"? There is a feeling in the Mass today that we shouldn't mess with the words, just do them as they are given.

The Mass in a Linear Perspective

Over the years, we have found it common in the Church to analyze the Mass in its parts. However, most of the time, we do so in a linear, horizontal fashion: first, a confession of sins, then readings from the Scriptures, followed by a homily and prayers of the faithful, etc.

This approach leads us to consider the symmetry within the Mass, how the first half connects to the second, how the lifting up of the book of the Gospels mirrors the lifting up of the bread and wine and the lifting up of the Body and Blood of Christ, and how the sharing of the Word reflects the sharing of the gift of the Eucharist to us. All of which is most enriching to us, for sure.

The Mass, Vertically, Reaching Downward to its Heart

Adding to that horizontal perspective, I believe it would be even more fruitful for us to look vertically, reaching down into the depths of the Mass, in order to see what might lie at its deepest levels, not looking at what merely comes next, but what exists at the levels deeper in the experience, to try to find what might be at the deepest core of the Mass, a look rather at the timeless essence of the Mass.

Converts frequently tell us that one of the critical moments for their turning to Catholicism was the experience of the Mass. Often they will witness to the mystery that they experienced, that there was something they couldn't find words for, and that they wanted to be in touch with, again and again. What they found, and what keeps us celebrating the Mass, is that same experience for which we often lack words to define.

The best example I can recount about this mystery is the silence that occurs again and again in the Mass. Occasionally it is breathtaking. In the midst of a homily, I look around at the absolute silence, as the assembly seeks to absorb the mystery that the homily seeks to convey.

Within the Eucharistic prayer, at the consecration, in the silent moments after Communion, you can sense that this silence is different from the silence which we might call "the absence of sound." This silence is steeped in meaning, pouring out of the assembly, something almost alive in itself, a virtual suspension of time and place, all of creation holding its breath in the presence of something greater. What is this all about?

The Silence at the Core

The bedrock of the Mass is a silence. That silence underlies everything: the Word of God, the action, the prayers, and even and especially the Communion. The silence of the Mass is not an empty silence, not like the silence in the contemporary world that needs to be filled with noise and should be, because for the most part it is a world afraid of any silence. The silence of the Mass is also unlike the kind of silence that death and loss bring upon us, the voice that is gone, the touch we've lost. Not that kind of silence either, not the silence of loss.

No, the silence of the Mass is rich and enveloping. It is a silence beyond words, when even words are not enough to express the meaning of the moment. In the Mass it is a silence laden and enfolded, a silence that we can't get enough of in our hearts and in our lives.

At the same time, the silence of the Mass is not expressive of something above and beyond us. Mystery here is not the unknowable, but the knowledge of revelation. There is content, even if there are not words, and there is meaning, even if it leaves the heart saturated or at a loss. The silence of the Mass envelopes us, and we can't quite get our arms around the moment. Such silence is nonetheless laden with content, a surprisingly relevant, spiritual content that strikes us in our very heart.

The music and the prayers, the words and the actions of liturgy do not contradict the silence, but rather point to it, drawing us further and deeper into that for which words are inadequate. Almost everyone who participates in a Mass has experienced their mind wandering to areas of the past week, of what hurts in their lives, of whom they should pray for, of those that they love who have died but with whom they remain united. If we reach that silence, we often know what in our lives need to change, or who it is that we need to reach out to. Yet as it is wordless, the silence is how the Spirit speaks, and we hear not with our ears, but with our hearts.

Often people tell me of a sense of guilt for not paying attention to the Mass. People apologize for being distracted at Mass. Frankly, I doubt that our minds wander that much, they are simply going to places where their time during the week would not allow them to access. Then when Mass begins, the Spirit opens us to vistas normally closed to us, and then draws us into subtle forms of contemplation. In a sense the Mass is a call to reflect on what's important in our lives and those things with which we struggle. Again, at its deepest levels the Mass is most often wordless.

Within the Silence, There Is Still More

Silence is not the end of the depth of the Mass, however. There is something at the core of the silence, enfolded in that silence. It is the reason for the silence, something that there are not words for, that leaves us struggling to grasp.

Enfolded in that silence is a moment, a context, a wordless dialogue that encapsulates the final moment of Christ on the cross, in His total abandonment to death, when Christ is lifted up to the Father in perfect humility, poverty and obedience, as an offering in exchange for us. At the very same moment, there is an acceptance by the Father in total love for the Son, and therefore, for us as well.

That moment is a fulcrum of the entire Mass, and that moment is most revealed at the point of the great Amen of the Eucharistic prayer, when the priest celebrant raises the Body and Blood of Christ and proclaims, "Through Him and with Him and in Him, all glory and honor is yours, for ever and ever." Every part of the Mass hangs on that moment. The consecration leads to that moment, the Communion draws from that moment. That moment is the fulcrum of everything.

Within That Moment, There Is Still More

Here is the context of that moment. The cross can only be understood in terms of love, the love between the Father and the Son, a combined love above all for humanity. In the climactic instant on the cross, Christ yields all that He is and has into the abyss. You can almost visualize the moment, Christ in His total love, somersaulting, twisting and turning as He crashes into the gates of hell, shattering totally the enmity of God and humanity.

On the Father's side, there could have been a breathless moment when it was in the Father's reach to determine whether or not to parlay the perfect sacrifice of Christ into the salvation of the world. Certainly, humanity and the world were not deserving of any of this love. Humanity was the reason for the crucifixion; humanity was under the power of sin. There were no redeeming qualities in humanity, nothing on our own to merit what transpired. Yet in that moment salvation, redemption, reconciliation, and all of the Father's love came to us. What the Father did for us is infinitely beyond our comprehension.

All through the religions of the world, up to and virtually including Judaism, God was not referred to as a God of love, but rather of justice, even of vengeance or punishment. There are traces of that love in Judaism, but they are often layered over by the justice of God. Only in Christianity can God truly be called the God of love, as He is by Saint John in his version of the Gospel and in his letters. The cross irrevocably defined that love, and swept us up with Christ into the arms of the Father. That love is asymmetrical over against the judgment we deserved.

It is all one moment, timeless and instantaneous, perfect love between the Father and the Son, all of which encompasses our souls. It is the completion of all time's preparations, the fulfillment of the ancient plan of salvation. Nothing could have blocked this love between the Father and the Son.

It is that moment of the cross that we hold in the silence of the Mass, a moment preserved and nourished in the depth of that silence, enfolded and wrapped in the most precious of ways for the present.

Time and the Eucharist

Time is arrested in the liturgy of the Mass, stopped, stalled in its tracks, in the moment of total giving on the cross, between the Father and the Son, a moment extended for all of two thousand years. It is celebrated in the great Amen at the conclusion of the Eucharistic prayer, those ten seconds when the priest lifts up the Body and Blood of Christ to pray for the whole community:

> Through Him, with Him and in Him,
> Almighty God and Father,
> in the unity of the Holy Spirit
> all glory and honor is yours
> forever and ever. Amen.

Those ten seconds always bring me to a final awareness that, even though I am a mere instrument, a mere person lifting up the Body and Blood of Christ, somehow I have been assigned to elevate this moment before the assembly. In that moment of offering I know I can't draw any closer to the essence of the priesthood in this world. Those ten seconds get me to the very essence of what it means to be a priest in the Catholic Church. Those ten seconds, in my mind, are the high point of my fifty years of priesthood.

Beyond my role, those ten seconds are the deepest and richest seconds in the 21st century. Those ten seconds get us all, as Catholics, to the very quintessential heart of time and history, to the moment that changes everything.

For myself, I clearly know that what I am doing at that moment is central to all of our faith. However, while I am elevating the Body of Christ and the Blood of the Chalice, I am keenly aware of my life laced through with limitations and obstructions. Yet that is what I have been called to do in Eucharist after Eucharist. Not that I am intrinsic to the action, my presence at that moment is accidental to what is happening. I am simply there, lifting up that holy and transformational moment of the salvation of all mankind. So it is for everyone there. That's the reason for the silence, because the moment is simply beyond words.

From a subjective point of view, that moment comes close to defining one of the key characteristics of the priesthood. That moment is a model of all that the priest does in his ministry. I am simply lifting up the central moment of our redemption, allowed to lift up the key action of the cross, of when Christ in total abandonment yields it all in total surrender to His Father.

This moment also reveals a key characteristic of the faithful who are celebrating this moment. Those who are present at that sacred moment are seemingly and mysteriously present in two different ways. First of all, we are one with Christ, as He offers Himself to the Father in this act of total love: He has wrapped us in the arms of His love in this moment, making us indistinguishable from Himself and His sacrifice, providing us cover for all of our sinfulness, creating a new bond of unity within the love between the Son and the Father.

However, in the Mass we celebrate, we are also witnesses of Christ offering us along with Himself on the cross. Thus we stand within the moment between the Father and the Son, and at the same time, stand aside the moment witnessing ourselves being redeemed by the sacrifice of the Son, and accepted on the part of the Father.

Just as Mary and John stood before the cross, so we stand at that very moment, but with the knowledge that we die and rise with Christ, because Christ has carried us with Himself, who is the perfect gift and offering to His Father in heaven. It bears thought that we might be standing both within and witnessing from aside that sacred moment that so transforms who and what we are within the Trinity. No wonder we are so speechless in the Mass!

The Centripetal Force in the Mass

Here is another dimension of the central moment, that central pillar enshrined in the Mass. In the Mass, we are pulled, centripetally closer and closer into that central moment at the heart of the Mass.

Visualize concentric circles, if you will. The most external would be the liturgical year within which these mysteries circulate. Within that circle, there is the season of Lent as a second circle leading further inward. That season leads us to the next inner circle, that of the Triduum, the three days of Holy Week that bring us closer and closer to the central moment. Within the Triduum, then, we are brought to the hour of the cross, the hour for which the Father has sent the Son. Within the hour, then, is that central moment, the moment of complete and total self-sacrifice where the Son, having wrapped all of us in the arms of His love, yields Himself completely to the glory of the Father and to the throne of grace. That moment is at the absolute center of things, the instant of total self-giving of all creation back to the Father, joined to the simultaneous acceptance by the Father that is revealed to us in the resurrection of the Son.

That's the moment of the cross upon which everything in creation and history depends. That's the moment, then, that is present to us, or that we are present to, in every celebration of the Eucharist. That's the moment that is the heart of hearts for the mystery of our salvation. That's the moment when time stands motionless, is tipped on end so that it can be the portal to eternity for all of humanity. That's the moment which unites both Christ's dying on the cross, the acceptance by the Father, and the time in which the Mass is being celebrated. How unique and incomprehensible that moment is: time gathered from near and afar, standing on end here and now, the moment that reveals the totality of God's love.

11. The Extent of the Silence

> He said to them,
> "This is my blood of the covenant,
> which will be shed for many.
> Amen, I say to you, I shall not drink again the
> fruit of the vine until the day when I drink it
> new in the kingdom of God."
> Mark 14:24-26

Once when I was an associate missioner with Maryknoll Missioners, living in Korea, I attended an ordination of eight young Korean men to the priesthood, celebrated at Myeongdong Cathedral in Seoul. This cathedral was located on a ten-acre plot in the midst of twenty-story to forty-story skyscrapers, as well as a major retail shopping area.

In Korea, at the time of ordination, entire parishes from the home of the one to be ordained were in attendance, all arriving by chartered buses. One of those eight to be ordained was from the parish where I was working and living, Tandedong Parish, in Seongnam City. There were many from our parish attending. In fact, there were hundreds from each parish there that day.

Since the Myeongdong Cathedral in Seoul, Korea, could not seat such numbers, most were gathered in the ten-acre garden space that surrounded the church, listening to loudspeakers placed about the campus. The space was filled with statues and grottoes, flower and rock gardens.

Following the conclusion of the ordination and the celebration of the Mass, the newly ordained exited the church and moved to give first blessings to each parish cluster gathered around them in the garden area. Each parish and their newly ordained were arranged there in the garden area kind of like bouquets themselves.

Even though there were several thousand there that day, the silence of those moments by the Korean Catholics was astounding. I have never heard such silence in my life; it embraced everything. It was a breathless moment, an extension of the ordination Mass and the sacredness of ordination to the priesthood for the Korean Church.

Even more astounding, this cathedral is located deep in the midst of one of the busiest shopping areas in that country, or equal to any other country. That means noise! That famous area was inundated with sound, with never a moment of quiet, with restaurants, up-scale department stores, and capped with thousands of people mingling on its streets. Buses and taxis were bumper to bumper. The lights never went out, the billboards sparkled through the night. It was a neighborhood that never slept. The closest thing to that center here in our country would be a day at the state fair in my home state with its thousands. A day there in the Myeongdong neighborhood went on every day throughout the year.

On that day of ordination, the silence of those several thousand Catholic parishioners overwhelmed all the noise of those that surrounded the cathedral. The silence was stunning and it resonated through the assembled faithful. Yet one hundred yards away, there was this cacophony of sound and the noise of the milling crowds and with all the noisy traffic. Even thirty years later, the memory of that day and that contrast still overwhelms me.

The Silence and the Noise

I believe that the day at the Myeongdong Cathedral can stand as an analogy of what is happening every time we celebrate Mass together in this age of nihilism. There is this moment of silence that underlies everything. There is this central moment, and when we sense its meaning, we are brought to a kind of total stop within ourselves.

Yet the secular world spins onward, following no plan or purpose, without any spiritual content, noisy and competitive, blind and lost. There is no room for silence in that world, as silence there is terrifying. It judges humanity without words. Such silence cries out for something to complete or fulfill life, and nothing does.

However, the silence of the Mass is exactly the opposite of this world, because its silence is filled with peace and forgiveness, with a joy and awe of what is transpiring in the central moment of the liturgy.

Vertical Time

Once we have found this central moment of the cross and of the Mass we can begin to express what that moment represents for us. The moment when Christ's sacrifice is completed, and simultaneously consecrated by the Father is the moment when all time stops, when all of creation's story changes, when everything shifts from shades of black and gray to a cornucopia of technicolor for humanity and the world. In that moment all the sin that has broken and fragmented humanity from the day of Adam to the end of this world is redefined in the love between the Father and the Son. And, we are there!

In the Mass, time is set on end. Past and future are joined to the present, and time is no longer horizontal, but is vertical, linked to eternity. In a shift of dimensions, in the Mass we are brought to that eternal moment in a spirit of awe and astonishment, despite the story of our bent and chaotic lives!

Place as Universal as Time

Place is equally irrelevant. It can be the smallest of chapels or the largest of churches, but the moment remains the same, the same place as Golgotha. It is not the architecture of the church that arrests us. It is Christ giving Himself to the Father, and the simultaneous response of the Father to His Son, and thus to us as well.

This moment puts us in a new and unique place within this world, and allows us a new kind of silence, one not of emptiness, but of completion, one not of isolation, but of belonging both to our God and each other. In that moment we are kneeling or standing, and we know where we are, who we are with, and most of all, what our God has done for us. This moment then is a silence unlike any other, a silence beyond words or definition, but packed with significance and mystery.

The Final Word

No wonder the world misreads what the Mass truly is. We cannot enter fully into the Mass without encountering this kind of silence. If we are in flight from ourselves, if we are grasping for something to hold on to in this world, it would indeed be scary to be dropped into the silence at the heart of the Mass.

On the other hand, when we have had enough of the emptiness that this world dishes out, when we have tried everything else, when we are sick of trying to live by our own wits, the Mass at its heart becomes a resting place for us and a moment to recognize the new reality that lies within us.

The Mass is a silent testament against what this world has become, a proclamation of all the hope that can exist in today's times. In this culture, the Mass no longer speaks from a commanding position, but rather stands silent and humble before God the Father.

This is our true power in the world. This is what will take down the agnosticism of our times. This is the undeniable truth that the Mass has to share, and it is done with silence first and foremost.

The Word of God was proclaimed through Moses and the Prophets, and all awaited the final Word, the dying and rising of Christ. That final Word is offered in stillness, when all the words of the Old Testament, as well as all the words of proclamation about the Word of God were not enough. Only in the silence of the cross was the ultimate Word spoken. No other word was necessary. No other word could match the silence of the cross. In the moment of silence of the Father and the Son at the juncture of the cross, the absolute final Word was spoken. In the Eucharist, we are brought to that moment. No wonder we can only properly define the Mass except with silence at its center.

12. The Bread of the Eucharist

> I have been crucified with Christ; yet I live, no longer
> I, but Christ lives in me; insofar as I now live in the
> flesh, I live by faith in the Son of God who has loved
> me and given himself up for me.
> Galatians 2:19-20

The bread that we use is one of the curious things about the Mass. This bread is so simple. It is the absolute minimum of the definition of bread. It is so little of the essence of bread that it is almost not bread. The bread of the Eucharist is just barely able to be defined as such. Flour and water, no salt, no sugar, no yeast, barely recognizable as such, if at all.

One would almost expect that in a liturgy as significant as the Mass, the main symbol, the main analogy used to spotlight the mystery ought to be more, not a minimum. Shouldn't the bread be a kind of artisan bread? What's going on here?

The "Breadness" of Christ

In essence this minimum of "breadness" is about the heart of the mystery of Christ offering Himself to the Father. Jesus is so stripped on the cross, not just physically, but spiritually due to the spiritual pain of bearing our sins, that He is at the absolute minimum of humanity, unrecognizable and undefinable in his humanity. He is absolute humility, total simplicity in His obedience to the will of the Father, that He should offer Himself for all of humanity in this fashion. Here He is, the King of the universe, the Son of God, the Judge of the world, reduced to nothingness, or at least the closest thing to nothingness, yet still human. He could not have lost more of His humanity and still have remained that person called into being by the Holy Spirit and born of the Virgin Mary. His nothingness was absolutely pure and totally holy.

It is as if, in His action on the cross, He reached the point that He so gave glory to the Father, that there was nothing left of Himself, that He reduced Himself to total emptiness so that only the Glory of His Father remained. Christ became that little fragment of bread that was reduced to almost total indefinability. All that was left was the total glory of His Father. No wonder it was enough for the forgiveness of sins, for the salvation of the world, for the redemption of souls. In this regard, no better symbol of Christ's sacrifice could be given in the Mass but the symbol of bread, reduced to its absolute minimum.

The Emptiness of the World and That of Christ

Perhaps it would help to reflect for a moment on the two kinds of emptiness that I am writing about. There is the emptiness and hollowness that is the result of a postmodern world, where there is simply nothing at all, nothing to hold on to, nothing that ranks above anything else. That emptiness of secularism is simply the content of all existence, devoid of any meaning beyond that of this material world.

Perhaps we could put secularism in slightly different terms. The secular world in which we live is like a container filled with emptiness. There is no truth. The self is simply a brand, a pretend reality, revised at a whim. There are no enduring values. Morality is what you can get away with. It has all been deconstructed. This is a complete emptiness. In the words of Hamlet, a "quintessence of dust, filled with sound and fury, signifying nothing."

Then there is this emptiness of Christ on the cross. Christ is literally poured out until there is nothing left of Him. Yet His emptiness is very different from that of our modern times. His emptiness is full of love for the Father, as well as for us. All is poured out to the glory of God the Father. His emptiness is full of focus and purpose. Christ's hollowness is not a void; His abandonment reaches across eternity, and yields absolutely and completely to the will of the Father. He leaves all behind in order to have ownership of the Father's will here and now.

On the cross, Christ takes humanity, as it is in Him, to the absolute zero of humanity. He could not have been less human, and still be fully human, when He gave Himself up in sacrifice to the Father for us. However, in that absolute zero of humanity, the love of Christ reached infinity. This was a kind of absolute inverse proportion of a kind never seen in all of history. That zero reduction of Christ's humanity allowed for a love sufficient to touch every part of humanity, reaching from Adam and Eve to the final coming.

The world of Christ on the cross is very different from that of secularism. Christ is reduced to nothingness, not clinging to His divinity, and having been stripped of His humanity. Yet even in His nothingness, He is not empty. Instead He is filled with love, love that is overflowing to the point of inundation. His is a love totally given to the Father, leaving nothing in Himself but that love. His is a love totally offered up for us, for all of humanity, above all, rich in His nothingness on the cross. His is a love that supersedes all of the sin and worthlessness of human life in a cascade of humility and obedience, shining in goodness to the ultimate degree.

Love and Freedom in Christ

If you visualize the freedom that Christ surrendered upon the cross, first setting aside His divinity, then giving up virtually all of His humanity, one might think that He had totally lost His freedom in being nailed to that cross. However, the moment when He yields everything over to the Father is His greatest moment of freedom, simply because it is His greatest moment of love for us and for His Father in heaven.

The freedom with which humanity has been endowed is primarily the freedom to love, nothing less. The love of Christ in that moment on the cross could not have been exceeded. It was the ultimate in love. Thus, the ultimate in freedom! Once again, how different from secularism's freedom that ends in slavery to Satan's inverted, alternative universe.

In terms of the freedom of our secular world, it was total loss of freedom for Christ on the cross. Pinned immobile there on the cross, no one could have seemed more helpless. Again it was the ultimate of immobilization, to the point of death, that liberated the Holy Spirit into our world in the absolute love of Christ for us. His love knew no bounds in an absolute freedom of the Spirit. Any other kind of freedom that may have existed is now obliterated in this one act of love. Now only one kind of freedom, that of Christ's, is worth living for or dying for.

In Philippians 1:21, Saint Paul says, "For to me life is Christ." It appears that Paul is well down the road to having become, as he says elsewhere, "in Christ."

Throughout all of our Christian history, we have been trying to define how we relate to Christ, the risen Lord. Saint Francis of Assisi suggested that we become another Christ. Venerable Bede wrote of the Imitation of Christ. Saint Patrick, in his breastplate wraps Christ around us, above, beside, below, and behind us.

But always we are less than in total unity in Him. In each of these examples, we are separate souls, standing outside of Christ. Only Saint Paul goes the rest of the way. His life is Christ; he is in Christ, in a total kind of freedom joined to the freedom of Christ, now showered upon creation by His one act of perfect love.

Hope Lies in the Eucharist

Paul's definition goes way beyond what seems humanly possible. In fact, it is pretty much beyond us. We have too much of self in us. We are ruled in part by all our desires, our yearning for a freedom quite different from that of Christ's. We are a nest of the seven capital sins. How could we ever be "in Christ"? Then we see the extent to which Christ went in His sacrifice to the Father, and we wonder how could we ever do even a part of that. We even wonder how we will get to heaven, if we have to divest ourselves of our egos and our desires. How will we ever let go of the will that seems to make us who we are in this world? Total humility and simplicity so easily escape us.

However we are not without hope. Christ gave us the Eucharist. He initiated the Mass so that we might day by day, and step by step, draw nearer and nearer to being in Christ. Every time we receive Christ into our hearts at Communion, that moment indelibly has an effect, that the Body of Christ becomes one with the person receiving Him. The Christ that we receive is the same one dying on the cross in total humility and simplicity, in a nothingness of total love, and He is planting that seed deeply within us in the Eucharist.

The blood we receive in Communion is the same blood that poured out of the side of Christ on the cross, transforming us at the deepest levels to trust our destiny and purposes to life in Him. No, Christ's gift of Himself to the Father is not out of range for us, but is constantly deepening inwardly within our souls, through the reception of his Body and Blood.

Every time we receive the Body of Christ, we should look carefully at the absolute simplicity of what lies behind what looks like the minimum of bread, but is really the perfect medium for Christ to assist us on our journey toward Him, divesting ourselves of this world and drawing us outside of our fragmented and flawed lives into the unity of Christ. The bread looks like poverty, almost nothing. The bread looks like slavery, a denial of freedom. It is, in fact, wealth and mystery beyond anything of this world. It is true freedom. It is true completion deep within our souls.

13. The Moment to Which and from Which All Flows

> And he was transfigured before them, and his clothes became dazzling white, such as no fuller on earth could bleach them. Then Elijah appeared to them along with Moses, and they were conversing with Jesus.
> Then Peter said to Jesus in reply, "Rabbi, it is good that we are here! Let us make three tents: one for you, one for Moses, and one for Elijah." He hardly knew what to say, they were so terrified.
> Mark 9:2-6

The distance is immense between the times we are living in and the Mass that we participate in. Let me illustrate. In the consecration of the bread and wine in the Eucharistic prayer we come across two participles: "given up" and "poured out," both used with the future tense.

After that, the celebrant says, "Do this in memory of me."

I used to think that those final words were somehow about just the action that Jesus was about to take on the cross, since he was speaking at the time of the Last Supper.

I had not looked deeply enough. Later I realized that Jesus was pointing the disciples, not just to the moment of crucifixion on Golgotha, but also to every instance of the celebration of the Mass. In addition, I don't believe that Jesus was distinguishing between the moment of the crucifixion and the moment commemorated at every Mass. They are the same moment, as if time has become elastic, stretched through the centuries to allow us to be present at the most sacred moment of all of revelation, or to allow that moment to be present with us today. This moment is the climactic moment that changes everything, that undoes the sin of Adam and opens the way to eternal life.

Those two participles, "given up" and "poured out," seem to describe an omni-directional event. First a body is given up to the heavens, then blood is poured out on the ground. There is a further sense of completeness, that nothing more could be offered than what Christ is offering now at this moment. His offering exhausts description, and defies any ability to get one's arms around it.

The Sacrifice Given Up and Poured Out

Those words convey also the sense of sacrifice, that what is highest in value in all creation is for Christ to give Himself as a sacrifice, every ounce of Himself given up and poured out.

This is always where the postmodern world parts company with us. Sacrifice is contradictory to everything that the egocentric world treasures. Sacrifice is pure foolishness. If there is nothing in the world but what we can see, and nothing in life other than what I can take in my short time within it, What purpose could sacrifice warrant? Also, to whom would such a sacrifice be offered? Certainly not to a God that doesn't exist, who never was, and never will be! In such a constellation, sacrifice is absurd.

There is also the little piece of who it is that is making the offering, the sacrifice. Our world would tell us that Jesus was just a man, nothing more. Granted that He thought that He was doing something special, but in the eyes of our era, it was really a waste of a life, as He was just a nobody, one among the millions who lived and died in this world. There is no awareness of who it is that is the sacrifice, the Son of God, sent into our world on our behalf, no sense of His mission, His destiny, His obedience, His purpose in coming. It was precisely for such a moment that He offers Himself, in exchange for us, totally and completely out of love for His Father in heaven.

Yet here we are, as Catholics, celebrating week after week a moment of total sacrificial giving, where we are present with Christ, the Son of God, when He offers Himself on our behalf given up on the cross and poured out in blood for our salvation. In the Mass is where we become witnesses to the Father's acceptance of the totality of Christ's gift to the Father on our behalf. From the moment of the crucifixion through the years since, we stand before that moment when all is changed due to the event of giving absolutely everything on the part of Christ to make this happen.

The Blood of Sacrifice

The Blood of Christ is one of the elements that can help us understand the extent of the reality of Christ's act on the cross and that we celebrate in the Mass.

Nothing is more vital than blood. Nothing is more vital spiritually than to receive the Blood of Christ. It is not different or additional blood that somehow appears in the Mass. It is the very same blood, not other, not additional, but the actual Blood of Christ that dripped down on the ground from the wounds on the cross and was poured out from His side for us, under the form of wine. That is the blood that we receive in the Eucharist.

Could anything be more breathtaking? It is not just poured out of His body, it is poured out to us even as it is offered to the Father for our sins. The consecration and the Communion frame that great moment of the conclusion of the Eucharistic prayer. One leads to it, and the other flows from it.

When Will This Sacrifice Happen?

At the end of the consecration, Jesus commands, "Do this in memory of me." It is an action we are to do. Christ's action is about those two participles "given up" and "poured out." This is the continuing action that forms the action of two thousand years of the Mass. That sacred moment of the cross where Jesus is given up in sacrifice and His blood is poured out upon the cross is the action that we complete each time in the present in the celebration of the Eucharist. There is no greater sacrifice, no more complete realization of the love between the Father and the Son, and their combined love for us than to do this in memory of Him.

Be clear, each Mass is not another sacrifice given up, nor another pouring out of His blood. It is the one moment on the cross both then and now. It is in the presence of Mary, John, and the holy women gathered before the cross, along with us witnessing that eternal instant of the salvation of the world. Time is abrogated and embargoed, to allow for the eternal to be here and now. There is only one moment of sacrifice of the cross, and it is here and now, as well as then at the place of the skull, Golgotha, as well as before that, in the Last Supper. Each are all the one moment.

The blood in the chalice at Mass is the same blood dripping down upon the ground at Golgotha. The Body of Christ with us under the form of bread is the Body of Christ bleeding that blood. And behind and within is that astounding instant when all is healed and reconciled with us now and then, in the unity of the Son and His Father, and as a result for us all.

At the end of the Eucharistic prayer comes the summary of that climactic moment. The priest holds up the bread and wine, become the Body and Blood of Christ, saying the words:

> Through Him, with Him and in Him, Almighty
> God and Father, in the unity of the Holy Spirit
> all glory and honor is yours forever and ever.
> Amen.

It is such a simple ending to the long Eucharistic prayer. At that moment, I know that the Father is accepting the sacrifice of His Son with an absolute and priceless depth of love that spills over into the human race for all time. Each time, I catch my breath. I don't deserve to be there.

Our task as disciples is to always give up the mysteries that lie within us in a complete offering to God and to pour out everything and all that is within us as a part of this great moment. We join our present moment to the great and universal moment of the cross.

One of the prayers in my life has always been that sometime, perhaps in eternity, at a heavenly celebration, I might have the privilege of standing next to the Blessed Virgin Mary, unnoticed but beside her at a heavenly liturgy, just to be close. I had thought that that would be the highest honor.

Just a silly yearning on my part! Only later, when I understood that central moment in the Eucharist better, I realized that, if in the Mass we are present at the moment of Christ's offering of Himself to the Father on the cross, Mary is also there with us, just as she is at the moment of the crucifixion. Thus, my prayers have already been answered. I don't have to wait or hope for that privilege. We stand next to her in each and every celebration of the Eucharist.

Moses, a Model of What Was to Come

An image: that of Moses arguing with God to save his people when God has considered wiping them out because of their sins.

> Moses implored the Lord, his God, saying, "Why, O Lord, should your wrath blaze up against your own people, whom you brought out of the land of Egypt with such great power and with so strong a hand? Why should the Egyptians say, 'With evil intent he brought them out, that he might kill them in the mountains and exterminate them from the face of the earth'? Let your blazing wrath die down; relent in punishing your people." (Exodus 32:11)

Clearly, here Moses is a type of Christ, as Christ on the cross is the only thing preventing the wrath of God toward humanity's deserved condemnation. Christ trades places with us, in a holy exchange, as if to say to the Father, that there is worth in all of us, that He finds us significant enough to die for. This is the exact moment to which and from which everything flows. Each Mass we celebrate centers itself around this moment, this surprising reversal of course, this absolute rescue of us by the Blood of Christ wherein the Father acknowledges and blesses the centrality of Christ for all humanity. This moment is the moment of our redemption, our salvation, and the certainty of our hope.

A Final Image: The Fiery Chariot of Elijah

There is a reference in the Old Testament, from the Book of Sirach that can highlight for us an image of the absolute and commanding moment that we celebrate in the Mass, that Christ experienced on the cross and offered in the Last Supper. That image is this, describing the death of Elijah, who is such a type of Christ Himself:

> You were taken aloft in a whirlwind of fire,
> in a chariot with fiery horses.
> You were destined, it is written,
> in time to come to put an end to wrath
> before the day of the LORD,
> To turn back the hearts of fathers toward their
> sons. (Sirach 48:11-12)

When we focus on that absolute and final moment of Christ's self-giving and the Father's acceptance of that gift, that climax of all of history, we see the love of Christ and the love of the Father for His Son, so complete and unlimited that we can know that this love is the Holy Spirit Himself.

Imagine, if you will, the point of completion of both our salvation and the origin of the resurrection: Christ borne like a whirlwind of fire, in a chariot with fiery horses, into the arms of His Father, along with the final inclusion of all humanity with Him into the core of this mystery of the Trinity.

Could anything more emphatically estimate this astounding central moment of the crucifixion—extended to each and every Mass we celebrate—this stunning moment of victory that changes all of history? The action of that central moment, that victory in the face of the defeat engineered by Satan exceeds the entire universe with the fire of divine love.

This is the moment in the Mass that we simply can't get our arms around. This moment is that which, if we truly grasped what was happening in the Mass before our very eyes and hearts, can give us now the power to face whatever challenges this secular world can muster.

This moment of the cross and the Eucharist, if we own it, is the defining moment of our faith. This moment encases the mysterious silence of the cross that frames our deepest understanding, the mystery to which we are called to participate. This is the astounding moment, as dramatic and final as the image of Elijah, as it were, in a fiery chariot, defeating even death itself, annihilating the gap between heaven and earth, between humanity and the Trinity.

14. What Happens to Us in the Mass?

> On the evening of that first day of the week, when the doors were locked, where the disciples were, for fear of the Jews, Jesus came and stood in their midst and said to them, "Peace be with you." When he had said this, he showed them his hands and his side. The disciples rejoiced when they saw the Lord. Jesus said to them again, "Peace be with you."
> John 20:19-21

Unlocking Our Hearts

My father once told me this story. He was the maintenance head of a major milk processing company after the Second World War. He said that one of his workers then seemed to have a special skill. That man could unlock any door in the building, without having keys for it. His ability to open doors seemed almost magical. My father once asked him how he came about that skill.

The man replied that he was a part of a special group in the military, that during the Second World War, especially after the Normandy invasion, was sent on ahead of the allied soldiers to unlock doors of buildings within France and Germany. He said that they were not to engage the enemy, but simply to open doors, so that when the regular soldiers came, they would immediately have access to every possible hiding place of the enemy. Thus they were trained as locksmiths.

The story has always fascinated me, not because of the mechanics, but rather because I sometimes believe that something similar has been our challenge spiritually. Our hearts often begin locked up, as it were, refusing access on the part of Christ, to make us grow and change. Further, our growth and change usually comes in our accessing the mystery of the Mass.

The question then is, How do we open our hearts to Christ? And then once opened, How does the presence of Christ in the Mass bring about this growth and change in us?

The Yes that Opens Everything

The fact is, before we can access the mystery and revelation hidden in the Mass and that is likewise hidden within us, we need to learn to see with the eyes of faith. The eyes of faith begin with a sincere and deep "yes" to the call of Christ. Only when we turn our heart and soul in total openness to Christ, only then do the doors of mystery fly open to us. This yes is the foundation stone of our faith. With only this yes does the work of the Holy Spirit take over, opening the gates to what the eyes of faith can see.

Apart from that yes, we are left in the darkness of the world beyond redemption, left to navigate without compass or North Star to guide us. The yes to Christ always comes first. We celebrate our yes in the Eucharist, each time we approach the altar, every time we receive Communion. We renew our yes every time we receive the Sacrament of Confession. Our prayers always need to reflect that simple yes at the heart of our lives.

Until we articulate that yes, we are stuck, with a kind of blindness we can't overcome. The doors remain locked within. The more we guide ourselves without that yes, the less we see of the Kingdom of God, the more the darkness reigns.

Similarly, there is nothing but darkness then within ourselves. That yes becomes the key piece to completing the picture of ourselves as a person. That yes takes us beyond ourselves, and opens the doorway to what God, from our creation, has hidden within us, that part of ourselves that we call "Spirit." Also, it could be called the supernatural within us.

Apart from the yes to Christ, everything spiritual remains simply a stumbling block to a self-centered life that we would then seek to define by ourselves. As a result of an attempt to live without Christ, we experience over and over again lives that leave us hungry and empty at the end of the day. However, what that yes to Christ does to us is that it provides us with a lens to bring into focus all that is hidden in us that God has put into us at our creation.

The Yes that Does Not Narrow Us, but Widens Us

Here is another way of seeing that yes. Usually when we consider saying yes to what Christ would call us to, we somehow think that that yes is narrowing our choices downward, that we are just giving something up in order to satisfy what Christ is calling us to accept.

Of course, in the shallowest dimension of that yes, a yes to Christ does seem to require giving up something. A yes to Christ seems to invade our ego, our will, our self-centered expectations. We easily end up saying: "But what about me? What about what I want!"

However, a yes to Christ does not narrow our lives, but quietly explodes into a cornucopia of options that only Christ Himself could reveal to us, that only the Holy Spirit can introduce us to in our lives. Our yes to Christ becomes theological, transcendent, and opens to pathways above and beyond what we ourselves would have imagined.

Picture, if you will, a grandfather sitting with his family at Christmas or some holiday, looking around at his children, grandchildren, and even great-grandchildren, with noise and laughter filling the house, thinking "Where did all this come from? How did this all come about?"

Of course, it all began with a day of vows, before the altar, when he and his spouse had made a simple yes before Christ to live as husband and wife, "Until death do us part." The priest or vowed religious, looking back, sense a set of equivalent miracles that flowed from their yes to Christ.

A yes made before Christ and to Christ never fails to change us, to lift us above what we could have imagined, to invite us to new and different vistas in this world. At its deepest level, the yes to Christ opens us to the ultimate dimensions of divine love.

What happens when we combine that yes to our Mass?

To appreciate the power of the Mass to form and shape us, we can only turn to analogies. The real meaning of the Mass is hidden from the eyes of the world, and can only be seen indirectly. Analogy, as a help to our eyes of faith, can help us in seeing what it is that our celebration of the Eucharist is doing within us.

Analogy also gives us the ability to enter inside the Mass, to visualize the reality of what is truly happening when we celebrate this sacred liturgy. In the Mass, it is almost as if, that when we have entered into the mystery of the risen Christ, we are taken ever deeper into the mystery of mysteries, and as it were, transporting us to the very moment of the transformation of the entire world, of all of history.

In every Mass, with the help of analogy, it is as if we have discovered a hidden city that had been lost for eons, or that we had stumbled upon cave drawings that had been lost since the dawn of humanity, or that we are walking in the midst of a garden untouched by corruption or evil. We become, as it were, witnesses to the ascending and descending of angels that Jacob envisioned in his dream.

All of these kinds of moments coalesce in that central moment of the sacrifice of Jesus on the cross, and the simultaneous acceptance by the Father of His gift, breathtaking and breathless in that moment when all of history and all of time is upended.

How Christ in the Eucharist changes us! Since such changes are beyond our counting, we can only turn to some images, simple as they are, to try to get at the reality of what Christ's presence and union does in our hearts.

Here are a few analogies that tell the story of what happens within us when we are invested deeply in the Mass.

The Mass, as Hourglass

Visualize, if you will, an hourglass, as a symbol of the Mass. The sand of our lives, in the moment of the

Eucharist, pours through the narrow part of the hourglass, grain by grain. What emerges below the narrow part of the hourglass is the beginnings, again and again, of a new life, a life that has been stored up in our spirit from the moment of our creation in the mind of God, allowing us now to begin anew the days of our life, now with the presence of Christ enthroned as it were in our hearts.

This means that our lives become more and more deeply connected to that central moment of Christ's on the cross, giving Himself to the Father on our behalf, as well as the knowledge that we have of our Father's acceptance of Christ's offering. And so, we are always beginning anew, as we try to grasp what that central moment of love means for us. The Mass is a divine hourglass, and our lives are the sand pouring through it, remaking us, reshaping our lives, revealing the extent of love that is there.

The Mass, as Mirror

Most of us have had the experience of standing before a mirror, trying to discern just exactly who and what we are. We often don't like what we see. Often, in seeing ourselves something seems missing, that we ought to be more or better. The image on the other side somehow reveals all our past, our history, our failures.

The Mass itself is a kind of mirror, but of a different kind. The Mass reveals to us an identity that is inaccessible to the world, an identity only possible in Christ Jesus. In addition, when we look in this particular mirror, we find that Christ has seen in us something of infinite worth, something in us for which it was worth making a total sacrifice. In the Mass, as a mirror, we begin to see ourselves as complete in Christ, no longer by ourselves. We find there the true definition of person. We are united as one with the Christ who has sacrificed Himself beyond all love for us.

This redefines for us who we are, and what our worth is. The person we see in the mirror of the Mass is a person of purpose and destiny, because we are connected directly to the Son of God, who at the same time is one with His Father. In addition the two of them, joined in the oneness of love, the Holy Spirit, shower us with the gifts of that same Spirit. The Mass is a divine mirror that reveals to us the depth of our nature and being. Once again we are breathless.

The Mass, as an Eye of a Hurricane

I have often thought of the Mass as being like the eye of a hurricane. Like in the midst of a massive storm there is an eye of calm, wind having died down, the storm seemingly having disappeared. Birds trapped in the storm are known to fly to the eye for a time of safety. So the Mass is similar.

This center in the Mass is simply marked with the silence of the Savior of the world, giving Himself wordlessly to His Father, coupled with the wordless acceptance on the part of the Father, consecrating the humanity that had been so lost and without hope in history. At this center there is silence, there is calm, there is resolution of the age-old alienation between the Creator and the creature. The silence here is infinite, so is the resolution.

The Mass is such a center, a still point in a world that has gone crazy from trying to live in the hurricane, rather than at the center, lost in a whirlwind of activity, of media, of technology, of sheer chaos, a world drawing ever closer to being without ethics, without purpose or without hope. There is a contradiction here: trying to live at the speed of light, while what is required for our souls is stillness.

However, in the Mass, you arrive at the center, stepping beyond time, stopping and resting, where motion is at peace. The Mass is the moment that takes you to the moment of the cross, the moment when Christ in the Mass and the Father are at one in our redemption, the moment the Spirit is released upon us. At Mass, you have stepped outside of time itself into the center of eternity, the point where the risen Christ is visible to the eyes of faith. Once again, even though the doors seem locked, you find Christ standing in your presence saying, "Peace be with you."

The Mass, as a Gateway

A last analogy: the Mass is a doorway, a now unlocked door, pouring everything from this side of our lives into a new reality. In every Mass we are taken to that point, actually having nothing from within us to qualify for our entrance through to the other side. We lack every credential necessary for this entry, our sinfulness disqualifies us, our trail of failure and self-centered character.

All says we shouldn't be there at this gateway, at this open door. Yet we are! Christ carries us there within the cross, and in the very central moment of the Mass. The Eucharist itself is our passport to the other side. Only in the love of Christ and the response of the Father are we at this gateway, and that we are acceptable now, and we can know it. This image of the Mass suggests that the Mass itself is an action, of passing from the old to the new, from the fragments of our humanity into the beginnings of a consecrated life in Christ. Every Mass is a kind of dying and rising, but always with our hand in Christ's.

The Mass and Secularism

The more we understand what happens at the central moment of the Mass, the more we will be prepared to transform our everyday lives into the life of Christ. Secularism seems to be attempting to do everything possible to lock the doors of faith, with a spirit of materialism. However, the Mass in all its depth is transformative for our whole life.

To summarize, let's put it in the context of the Blood of Christ that we are to receive in the Mass. Visualize the Blood of Christ poured into your heart and soul at the moment of Communion. This is the blood pouring out from the side of Christ on the cross at each Mass. In essence it is poured out into us, mingling with our own blood, joining our own sufferings, transforming us to more closely resemble Christ.

If ever there was an image that can show us what is happening at Mass, it is the moment of receiving the Blood of Christ. It is, as it were, the Blood of Christ mingling spiritually with us into one! The action turns out to be within us, forming and shaping us into the image of Christ Himself, joining us irrevocably into one with the liturgy of heaven itself. The knowledge and understanding of all this starts with the deepest possible yes to Christ that we can make.

Even though the culture we live in is doing all it can to lock the doors of faith, Jesus comes, even though the doors are locked, and stands in our midst and says to us, "Peace be with you."

Then, the risen Christ opens for us both the mystery of salvation and the revelation of God's love for us, as well as our own intrinsic worth as God's children and creation.

15. Fathers and Sons: Reaching into the Central Moment

*"My son Absalom! My son, my son Absalom!
If only I had died instead of you,
Absalom, my son, my son!"*
2 Samuel 19:1

If we are thoughtful, one of the windows that opens for us in the Eucharist is the relationship of the Father and the Son. In the prayer of the great Amen, we come to a clear understanding of the Son, offering Himself totally and perfectly on the cross to the Father, and at the very same moment, witnessing the love of the Father overwhelming the sacrifice of the Son. Within that moment, flowing from it comes the love of the Father and the Son for each other that we know as the Holy Spirit, streaming and cascading from that moment into our hearts for all time.

The mixture of humanity and divinity here is astounding. Perhaps the only way to get to an understanding of the moment is to look at the relationships of fathers and sons in the Scriptures. Each one casts some light on that mixture.

We have a tendency to view that moment on the cross exclusively from the viewpoint of Christ's experience. That is understandable, given the graphic and horrendous nature of His death. Yet the Father's role and moment is equally overwhelming.

David and Absalom

Look for a moment at the relationship of one set of fathers and sons in the Old Testament. It is David and his son, Absalom. Absalom has betrayed David and carried out a palace coup to rid David of his throne. It was a huge betrayal, but David, despite being humiliated in his escape, never gave up hope. When the soldier brought word of Absalom's murder, shouting it as if it were a great victory, King David broke down in grief:

> My son Absalom! My son, my son Absalom! If only I had died instead of you, Absalom, my son, my son! (2 Samuel 19)

If David could have that depth of feeling for his son who had so severely betrayed him and sought to kill him, how much more could we see God the Father's response to the death of His innocent, humble, and obedient Son, murdered by rebellious humanity!

I know we don't attribute emotions to God the Father easily, but I also know that Jesus was not alone in His crucifixion and death, that His Father, albeit unseen, was a deep participant in that very moment of the death of His Son. That moment has been depicted as the throne of mercy.

We know from Jesus' quote from the Psalms, "My God, my God, why have you abandoned me?" that the isolation and emptiness of Jesus on the cross was more than anyone could measure.

Surely God the Father was an equal participant in that moment. The Father had to be, as it were, holding His breath, enduring His own kind of agony, that He had sent His only begotten Son to this moment. In contrast to David and Absalom, in the death of God's Son, the only betrayal was on the part of those for whom Jesus died. He died in innocence for us who were not so. This is mystery beyond mystery, hidden as well, deep within the Mass.

Abraham and Isaac

We catch a similar flavor from the story of Abraham and Isaac. God inexplicably asks Abraham to sacrifice his only son, Isaac, the very son who was such a miracle of conception and birth in the old age of Abraham and Sarah. When Abraham complies with God's request, God also inexplicably prevents the act of sacrifice at the last minute. The story through the centuries appears to be a test of faith and obedience on the part of Abraham. As such, it is a beautiful story, but one that in essence remains deeply puzzling with regard to God. Why give this son, and then take him away?

Only when we turn to the New Testament is there a new glimmer of light about what this story of the Old Testament might have been referring. Viewed from the moment of Jesus dying on the cross, all of a sudden, we can understand the Genesis story as a type of what was to happen, when in obedience of the Son to His Father, Jesus allows Himself to be led to the cross, and to die at the request of His Father. The Father allows His only Son to die for our salvation, as Abraham almost sacrificed his only son.

In essence it is about the will of God the Father, and the terrible price exacted for that which the Father and the Son would accomplish. And that moment sits at the exact center of the Mass. It is that moment that we are witness to at the conclusion of the Eucharistic prayer.

Jacob and Joseph

There is more, another father and son: Jacob and Joseph. Jacob was elderly, becoming blind if not already blind. His son, Joseph, was his favorite. However, due to his brothers' jealousy, Joseph ends up being sold as a slave into Egypt, saved from death by one of his eleven brothers, Reuben, and sold for 20 pieces of silver. The brothers reported back to their father that Joseph was dead.

We have little explanation of what Jacob, the father, endured, as a result of this loss. There must have been years of feeling this, unaware that it was a betrayal on the part of his other sons. Yet we see by the end of the story in Genesis that they are reunited in Egypt, father and sons, together with Joseph. The family is saved from famine, by the efforts of the son, who supposedly had died. Again, as with Abraham and Isaac, this story seems to point nowhere other than to what is contained within the context. It is a beautiful story about a father and a son, lost and found, apparently dead and now alive.

Imagine the moment of reunion between Jacob and Joseph, after all they had been through. Added to that, the life of Joseph, sold into slavery, brings salvation to all his brothers, who of course are carrying the guilt of their betrayal. This moment of reunion in Egypt becomes a type of the moment on the cross, when Jesus lays down His life totally and definitively in sacrifice, and union with His Father. Jacob and Joseph prefigure this aspect of Jesus and His Father.

On one side is the pain of the sacrifice, on the other is the embrace of the Father and the Son reunited. Joseph's brothers in their pain remind me of the apostles, carrying the guilt of having abandoned Jesus from the moment of His arrest. How like the eleven brothers.

This is simply another way to talk about the central moment of the death of Jesus, but also of that same moment celebrated in every Eucharist, in every Mass, a moment that we are attentive to, that seals the hope of every disciple of Christ. In that moment we know that our debt, beyond redemption on our part, is paid by the sacrifice of Christ, and accepted as full payment on the part of the Father. And we are witnesses to that very moment in every celebration of the Eucharist.

The Prodigal Son

There is another story of a father and his sons, in the New Testament, the parable of the prodigal son. The father in this parable does an interesting, but contradictory thing: when the son requests his portion of the inheritance, the father quietly complies. However, the father appears to realize what will happen with that inheritance, that it will be squandered. In addition, the father seems to be waiting the son's return. He literally places everything in the hands of the son, seeming to know what would happen.

I picture the father watching from the front porch, looking off into the distance for some sign of the son's return. He knows he has to return. When he does see him, he orchestrates a celebration regarding the return of his son.

This reunion is rich in symbolism for us. There is, of course, much more to the parable than this moment of reunion, but the reunion of father and son in the parable helps us to think about the central moment of Jesus offering Himself to the Father, an offering so deep that the just accusation and punishment of the sins of humanity can be set aside, as if the unfaithful son were actually Christ bearing us in our sins.

This moment of reunion in the parable also brings us to the same moment in the Mass when the offering of the Son to His Father is celebrated in total honor and glory.

There is an apocalyptic aspect to the story, where the miracle of the son's return becomes the feast with the fatted calf prepared in celebration. Sin has been defeated and wiped out by the cross; the sacrifice of Jesus upon the cross has paid the debt incurred by humanity, and the Father is rejoicing. The banquet follows, the Mass having been prefigured here.

Humility and Poverty, and the Trinity

Once more, with reference to the Mass, we more easily see the portion of our redemptive story from the standpoint of Jesus dying on the cross, exchanging places with us to pay the bill for our infidelity. What we should also recognize is the very moment in the Mass when we lift up the Body and Blood in a great, final conclusion of the Eucharistic prayer. There is also the simultaneous response of the Father consecrating and celebrating the action of His Son in calling Him to be raised from the dead. "This son of mine was dead, and has come to life again" (Luke 15).

When we consider the humility and poverty of Christ on the cross, celebrated in the Mass, the utter simplicity of his self-giving to the Father, we ought to consider from where those virtues come. These astounding traits originate not in the human nature of Christ, although they are certainly present. Rather, we find them first in the divinity of the Father and the Son. It is in the cross, and then in the Mass that we witness this total humility and poverty of the Son toward the Father, as well as the same qualities in the Father, allowing His Son to die for us.

The Father, as it were, allows this to happen, without anger, without retribution for what our sins have done to His beloved Son. There seems immense humility and poverty on the part of the Father as well, even if there is really no way we can see how the Father could be this way.

With this thought we are back to the moment of Abraham and his son Isaac that was so incomprehensible in the Old Testament. The absolute obedience and humility of Abraham mirrors the same trait in God the Father, except that this time, the Father goes all the way.

Who would ever describe God the Father in terms of humility and poverty, except after recognizing what the Father asked of His only Son, that His love went to the ultimate extreme in the sacrifice of His Son for us. The Father hovers over his dying Son, almost as if He were in mourning, as if experiencing such loss as His only Son.

We have often portrayed God the Father as all-powerful, all-knowing, all-everything. We forget what the Father did for us in the sacrifice of His Son. The Father seems to have turned everything upside down for the sake of His creation. It was total humility and poverty on His part, a humility and poverty as a divine attribute. That is astounding, and is incomprehensible that God might have reached this far for humanity.

The humility and poverty of the Son is equally spectacular. Just in the incarnation, being born as a human, He walked among us as a man. Then, seeing where that incarnation leads, that it passes through death itself, in a totally human display of humility and poverty, abandoning everything of His humanity to offer Himself to the Father on our behalf, in what seemed a total defeat as a criminal, unjustly accused and executed.

That sacrifice in human terms is as inexplicable as the step the Father took to bring about the redemption of His creation. This poverty and humility is rooted in the very nature of the Son of God toward His Father, yet is expressed through His full character as a human being.

The Love that is the Holy Spirit

The cross at this moment comes as close to defining infinity as is possible. You can look at it as an inverse proportion. The more the emptiness and humility, the further Christ descended into poverty and simplicity, the greater was His love manifested before His Father. That love on His part approaches and even exceeds infinity, as does His poverty in the other direction. In His total abandonment, we celebrate His total love. That love in its infinity is large enough to wrap every part of humanity into the love of the Father. No wonder His love is never exhausted. No wonder He is the Good Shepherd. No wonder He is "the Alpha and the Omega" (Revelation 22:13). No wonder the Father's acceptance of His Son's sacrifice is infinite!

As a result, from this exchange of humility and poverty, this exchange of selfless love, comes the beginning of the redeemed life, the way, the new creation that we celebrate in the Eucharist. Everything then flows in a perfect connection from the cross to the Mass in the present.

This is the moment in the Mass when all time is set on end. This is the moment when the Holy Spirit is released, when this absolute love between the Father and the Son is bestowed on our world. This one moment of all time persists as the presence of the Holy Spirit, through the ages, and consecrates the present in a totally new way, and we are there for it.

This moment on the cross also teaches us where such love comes from, the love that is divine. This divine love starts with humility and poverty and simplicity. Without those kind of elements, such love is impossible. The more we, as disciples of Christ, live lives that are humble, spiritually poor, and replete with simplicity, the more we are capable of Christ-like love.

There is no room for ego here, none to focus on self, either. To become like the Eucharistic bread, as humble as that bread, is the gateway to divine love in our lives. The power to live in that fashion flows directly from the most sacred moments of the Mass, as such humility and love is beyond what powers we have within ourselves. Only in Christ can we locate such love, and the deeper we go into that moment of the Eucharist the closer we come to those gifts that only Christ Himself can bestow.

What is more, the age in which we are living, the times so marbled through with its agnosticism and decaying morality, the only hope we have, in seeking to live with a Christ-like love, lies in this central moment that the Mass encapsulates. Everything flows from that moment. All the community, all the comprehension, all the courage needed for these times will become apparent if we take to the depths of this central moment around which the Mass itself is focused.

16. Unrequited Love

> See what love the Father has bestowed on us that we may be called the children of God. Yet so we are. The reason the world does not know us is that it did not know him. Beloved, we are God's children now; what we shall be has not yet been revealed. We do know that when it is revealed we shall be like him, for we shall see him as he is.
> 1 John 3:1-2

The First Person of the Trinity, whom Jesus taught us to identify as "Our Father," is central to the Blood of the Chalice that forms the heart of our faith life and the heart of the Eucharist. Most of the prayer of the Mass is directed to the Father. At times, this Father of ours is the one about whom we seem to know the least. Saint John, most of all, quotes Jesus often, saying, "If you know me, you know my Father." "I and the Father are one." Sometimes we see him as simply God, a kind of unknowable divine person, saturated in mystery.

We need to know Him better, as one deeply involved, as the one intrinsically instrumental, at the center of the mystery of our salvation and redemption.

Perhaps, we can most easily come to know our Father in heaven by understanding the experience of unrequited love, that is, one-sided love. In unrequited love, a person gives him or herself to another person in love, completely and without reservation, no conditions, no limitations at all. In authentic love, there is no such thing as forty percent, or seventy-five percent self-giving. If it is that, it is not love! The person who loves deeply pours it all out for the other, without knowing or seeing the response on the other side, by the one loved. No guarantees, no conditions, period! This leaves the person who loves vulnerable and in a spirit of complete trust that the love given will be reciprocated. Sometimes, it is not!

Unrequited Love in this Existence

Every parent, bringing a child into the world, experiences this one-sided love, yielding themselves totally to this newborn child they have just brought home for the first time from the hospital. A pregnant woman yields herself totally and completely to the child that she is carrying. In the birth of a child, there is no assurance that this child will reciprocate this love. Someday this child might reject a lifetime of love that has been given, and turn their back on the parent who has sacrificed so deeply in bearing and upbringing their son or daughter. At times, the parent feels this loss of love that they had so deeply invested in.

In a marriage, sometimes one partner will make a total investment of love in the other, while the other hides reservations and conditions to that response. Often that marriage does not go well, as a result, ending in some form of unreciprocated love. One loved with all his or her heart, the other dissembled, and after a time, the one-sidedness shows itself, almost as a kind of unbearable wound on the part of the one who loved completely.

The Father's Love

God the Father is the master/victim of unreciprocated love. From all eternity, climaxing in our creation, the Father has invested in us His endless and infinite love, hoping beyond hope that His creation would come and be one with Him in a free response of love back to Him, the Father.

As we know, it did not work out that way. The love of the Father was refused by all humanity, cascading down through the ages from the time of the sin of Adam and Eve, and that is now climaxing in the ways of our secular world.

The unrequited love of the Father is foreign territory here. Love that is given without guarantee of response usually leaves the lover vulnerable and open to impoverishment. And so it seems for our Father in heaven, who has loved us from all eternity. His love was left unreciprocated through the ages. Our Father in heaven was, as it were, abandoned, His love refused and rejected.

The Father's Unrequited Love for Us

This is not how we usually think of our God. We have been schooled in the attributes of God, as all-powerful, all-knowing, without flaw or weaknesses. Yet, in love, in the trust that love imposes, he seems to take on a vulnerability, a kind of poverty typical of the unrequited lover, similar to what we also can become in our thwarted attempts at loving. This is a kind of poverty that seems inappropriate or certainly surprisingly foreign to our image of God.

Thinking in this way almost redefines love as a kind of weakness, whereby someone gives away everything in an act of love, and then stands there alone, rejected, yearning for the one that has been lost. This reflection then also allows us to imagine our Father in heaven as the one who has lost us, and even to project on the Father a kind of pain of loss of His own creation. This image appears far distant from those divine attributes.

Usually theologically, we think of ourselves as being the ones lost to this world by virtue of our sins and pride, abandoned by God, His back turned from us as we choose sin rather than love. That is certainly the truth of the matter from one standpoint.

However, there is room to imagine the loss belonging also to the heart of our Father. Thinking in this way helps us to see our Father as the one who is taking an infinite step to find a way to bring us back, the extreme step of sacrificing His own Son in order to bring us back, of letting us know just how deep and all-encompassing His love is for us.

All this is beyond the pale, a kind of thought experiment that tries to reach somehow into the depths of what our Father in heaven, as it were, would feel for the experience of having loved us into existence, and then having found us wanting.

This can also help us to understand the commission and the call to obedience that the Father placed upon the Son, in sending Him into this world. Perhaps, part of the human response of Jesus to His Father in heaven could clearly have been to heal the loss of love that the Father yielded to in all humility and poverty, in His having loved His creation as He did.

I know that these words are reaching far into the subjective, suggesting almost that God would or could somehow have the same experience of love that we might have on being rejected or abandoned by the one we opened ourselves to in love. I am simply trying to put God's love in human terms despite the fact that our love is a mere shadow of what and how God Himself loves.

In addition, it suggests to me that attributes such as poverty and humility might not just be human traits, that in part, they might be divine traits. Since the Father and the Son are one, when Jesus suffers the ultimate impoverishment and humiliation that He did, He might also have been telegraphing to us that these characteristics are a part of our Father in heaven. It also suggests that those traits that we find almost human in our God might also be the most spiritual and redemptive things that exist in our nature, through the workings of grace.

The Father's Story of Our Lives

The story of redemption is a story of unrequited love, told from the viewpoint of our Father in heaven. It is a story that looks like there is pain on the part of our Father in heaven because of the loss of ourselves to Him. It is a story of a Father that never gives up on the return of His children to Himself. It is the story of a Father willing to try anything to bring us home again. It is the story of a father willing to sacrifice his son, Isaac, on mount Moriah, the story of a father having given his inheritance to an unworthy son, and then awaits his return, who when all else has failed, returns to seek forgiveness. Our redemption is the story of God willing to give up everything in a spirit of humility and poverty, even His own Son, in order to bring us home. How incomprehensible it all is!

I have a sense that many fathers in this world have struggled greatly with a son or daughter in their lives. Many have told me of their sense of poverty and humility in being a human father, about how easy it is to become estranged from someone you have loved for their whole childhood. In those cases, there is often a long time of waiting for the right moment to heal a breach, or to plot a fresh start with their child. It is part of what it means to be a father: to never give up on a son or daughter. Perhaps it's one of fatherhood's deepest traits, one of God's deepest, also.

The Divine Nature of True Love

We know from where that trait comes. It comes from above, from the deepest characteristics of our Father in heaven. It's all about love and forgiveness, healing and reconciliation, and these are things of the divine. It is about the Father's unrequited love for us. The extent of that love extends far beyond what humanity has deserved. How could he have loved this way? All of this takes our breath away!

This brings us to the love of Christ, given back to the Father on our behalf. This is the sacred moment on the cross, celebrated in the Mass, of the total love of Christ, given to the Father in perfect sacrifice and offering, given in such a manner that the completion of the circle of love, the other side of love owed to the Father finally fits irrevocably and neatly in place, never again to be breached. From the beginning, even before the beginning, from all eternity the love of the Father has been there, waiting, yearning for the return of His children. Now in Christ, the Father's love returning to Him in His Son knows no bounds.

Now the love between our Father and us, in Christ, is liberated. We can envision the love between the Father and the Son, the Son and the Father, as having no bounds, so powerful that the Holy Spirit of Love is now released on all of humanity that is open to accepting it.

That moment from the cross is the climactic moment of all creation. That moment is the moment around which we gather at every Eucharist. That moment is the absolute flow of love on the altar of the Eucharist, between heaven and earth. That moment is like a whirlwind of connection between the altar of the Eucharist and the heavenly altar, a tornado of love, spilling out into the time and place of every Mass, a tornado linking heaven and earth, time and eternity.

This is the strangest of love stories, impossible to have been imagined were we not experiencing it over and over in our lives and in the Eucharist. This is a story of love tipped on end, incomprehensible to the maximum, astounding to the mind. We are steeped in our own unworthiness, and shocked by the dimensions of our Father's love and the Son's obedience that rescues us from this impossible unworthiness. How far we are from the empty container of secularism, from the inverted, alternative universe of Satan.

17. Time, Upended

*Were not our hearts burning within us while he spoke
to us on the way and opened the scriptures to us?*
Luke 24:32

The Mass does something unique to time. In our lives there are certain events where time seems to stop, family celebrations, a moment of love, an awakening and the like. Time as it were becomes suspended in the intensity of the event.

In the Mass there is that intensity, but there is more. The only way I can describe it is to say that time is upended, and we are set crossways to the sequence of events. This time is expansive, including the past and the future in it. This is eternal time, the crossover to the kingdom of God. This is the place and moment where the risen Christ is most present.

> And it happened that, while he was with them at table, he took bread, said the blessing, broke it, and gave it to them. With that their eyes were opened and they recognized him, but he vanished from their sight. Then they said to each other, "Were not our hearts burning within us while he spoke to us on the way and opened the scriptures to us?"
>
> So they set out at once and returned to Jerusalem where they found gathered together the eleven and those with them who were saying, "The Lord has truly been raised

and has appeared to Simon!" Then the two recounted what had taken place on the way and how he was made known to them in the breaking of the bread. (Luke 24:30-35)

The hearts that were burning in the two on the road when Christ was present to them, that is the same moment within us when we grasp what is happening in the Mass, that Christ speaks to us, teaches us, and joins with us in the breaking of the bread. Often we experience such moments in the Mass, though we seldom have words for what is happening.

What Happens in the Breaking of the Bread

Sometimes a person seeking the faith is drawn to experience the Mass for the first time. Their experience often lacks words. There seems to be mystery here for which they can't account. Anyone who seeks the depth of the Mass, rather than just the sequence of events in the Mass, will find the door open to this hidden and inexpressible mystery.

We find ourselves thinking about people in our lives, reviewing our yesterdays, addressing our hopes and needs, often without a sense of where we are or what we are doing. We become so accustomed to the experience that we think it normal, even though it is anything but that. Rather, it is sacred mystery that we have been drawn into.

In addition, there is a dialogue happening in the Mass. We hear without words what the presence of Christ is teaching us. There are moments in the Mass that lend themselves to this experience. The risen Christ speaks to us, usually subtly, but with true effect. We become used to listening for those moments, hearing more than is said, listening to what is beyond the music or the silence.

This dialogue is a two-way street. It most often begins with us yielding our hearts and our lives to Christ, admitting our sins and failures, sharing with Christ the irresolvable obstacles that litter our lives. Our words set the stage. Each of us then has to discover the moments when the risen Christ speaks to us, sending His Spirit to dwell in us, and recalling for us the events and the truths that unravel the difficulties within us. Often this is so subtle that we are unaware that it is happening.

It has been said that the definitive Word has been spoken on the cross. That Word is the silence in the moment of the death of Christ. No more words are necessary. No word could exceed the Word of the cross, the sacrifice of Christ. That said it all.

At the same time, all of us can have an experience of the Word speaking directly in our hearts. The Mass, once we reach its depth, places a voice in our heart, drawing us into understanding and comprehension of all that is important to us. Every Mass should include careful listening for the wordless guidance and invitations that can only come from Christ. They are wordless, but you can hear them in the mystery of the Eucharist.

Jacob's Dream

One of the best descriptions of the Mass has been the passage regarding Jacob's dream.

> Jacob departed from Beer-sheba and proceeded toward Haran. When he came upon a certain place, he stopped there for the night, since the sun had already set. Taking one of the stones at the place, he put it under his head and lay down

in that place. Then he had a dream: a stairway rested on the ground, with its top reaching to the heavens; and God's angels were going up and down on it. (Genesis 28:11-12)

In the analogy of Jacob's stairway, with angels going up and down, something of the very essence of the Mass is captured, the Mass as the point of contact between us and the heavenly liturgy. The pathway is opened, and it is beyond time. Not just that time is stopped, but time just steps out of the way, and we find ourselves vertically connected between heaven and earth in a kind of non-time.

This is the pathway that the dying and rising of Christ has opened up. In that pathway, we come to a realization that our lives rise beyond the nitty-gritty of everyday life and are lifted to a different dimension. Somehow the events of our lives are relevant to what is happening in heaven and are on a journey different from that of worldly time. In truth, there are indeed angels going up and down between the earthly liturgy and the heavenly. It is the still point of this chaotic world.

Windmills and the Spirit of Peace

Windmills have become once again a normal thing in our daily American lives. They used to be ubiquitous in farm life, but today they are electric generators. We drive by them, as they seem to whirl slowly in the wind, as they generate electricity.

I was told once that the tips of the blades are actually not rotating slowly at all, but probably moving at a speed of almost 200 hundred miles per hour. I've tried to estimate if that speed is true, guessing that the tip of the blade is approximately five to seven building stories away from the center. Then I tried to time the revolution.

What I came up with was only another guess, but I know that the farther away the tip of the blade is from the center, the faster the speed. This also means that the center of the blades is moving very, very slowly, and that if we were to stand at the center exactly, impossible of course, we would be virtually motionless.

I often think of the Mass in those terms, with our daily life lived mostly at the tip of a whirling blade, swung around and around. We can barely catch our breath in our daily lives, a centrifugal force leading us in disastrous directions, nothing in focus, everything immeasurable.

Then in the Mass, we find that we are moving toward the center of the windmill, and that if we reach the center, we are motionless, in stillness, where everything takes on the dimensions of timelessness, where time is no longer horizontal, but is upended, beyond time, connecting us with the liturgy in heaven, bringing us to the depth of the cross, shaping us from within our relationship to the risen Christ.

I wonder if it is ever possible to bring our lives into focus without Christ. I think that only in Christ will we be able to clarify who we are and to where we are pointed. Only in Christ will we be able to measure our lives, to orient ourselves in either a sense of peace or in a grasp of truth. Once we find what is hidden deeply within the Mass, will we come to know who we are and why we are here. Only in Christ do we have the possibility of becoming whole in the midst of this fragmented and humiliating world of secularism. Why would we not turn to the Mass where we can forever witness the Christ who has given of Himself totally for us.

Part III

The Opportunities We Have

18. Hidden in Plain Sight

Think of what is above, not of what is on earth. For you have died, and your life is hidden with Christ in God.
Colossians 3:3-5

One of the remarkable mysteries of the present age is that the Mass itself is hidden from the world around it. It is not like it is some secret ritual, inaccessible to anyone who would seek to find it. In fact, the Mass in all its richness is simply hidden in plain sight. Even the name we give to the Eucharist, "the Mass" belies its sacred nature, and appears to be simply a word that is not even particularly descriptive of what it really is.

The Mass is only faintly portrayed in film or television these days, often a mishmash somewhere between a Protestant service and the actual Mass we celebrate. Usually in those instances they seek to portray a funeral or wedding, but they never quite get it right, or get to the core of what is happening at a Mass, the Scriptures, and the Eucharistic prayer leading to Communion. Just as well!

The media doesn't go there for very good reasons. One such instance of this disregard was a scene in a TV show, where the character, supposedly a Catholic priest, was dressed in a chasuble, the overall vestment that priests wear at Mass. This particular kind was commonly called a "fiddleback" and was very old fashioned. The vestment was to be square on the part of the priest's back, and the fiddle part was so curved, facing front.

You got it. For about ten minutes he was wearing the vestment backwards, and it was clearly awkward that way. Nothing could have been more inappropriate. Kudos to the actor, ignorantly dressed, who performed as if it were perfectly natural. How typical that they just don't get it. They never will in the media!

The Catechumenate of Old

Even in the early days of the Church, the catechumens were dismissed from the Eucharistic prayer and Communion of the Mass. They were asked to leave the celebration after the homily and the Creed. The mystery was reserved for those who had already gone the distance of being baptized and confirmed into the faith. Only those were invited into the depth of the mystery of the Eucharist. Today, despite our efforts at the renewal of the catechumenate, often no such dividing line exists in many parishes.

Instead, the mystery of the Mass lies hidden in plain sight. Anyone who hasn't turned their life over to Christ or sensed the risen presence of Christ in their midst is left with a void in their awareness.

Youth today, if they are really invested in the spirit of the times, or haven't found Christ in their hearts yet, simply see a boring hour wasted when on a Sunday morning they could have had another hour of sleep. Those for whom life centers around Saturday night activities easily see the Mass as a contradiction in their lifestyle. Sundays are for recovering from Saturday night. Weekends away, golfing, hunting, and fishing easily fill a life far distant from the sacred mystery of the Mass, crowding out a Sunday Mass from their experience. We will never comprehend what is happening if, in our list of priorities, Mass ranks way down the list near the bottom. The Mass has to be at the top of our list of priorities.

The Heart of the Matter

The heart of the matter is turning our lives over to the Christ in our midst, the risen Christ, the center of everything that matters. The Mass requires a deep awareness of the living Christ in our lives, with a total dedication to Him. Anything short of that awareness leaves us lurching around in the dark, fumbling at finding out who we are, wondering why our lives don't matter like they should.

There is no shortcut. We simply have to make Christ the center of our days and our lives. Everything else fails. The absence of awareness of the presence of Christ today is the reason things don't work for us. Without Him, we are fragmented and become victims of the evil that circulates around us in this culture. Without Christ, we are Satan's stooges, at risk for becoming participants in the inverted, alternative universe of Satan.

So therefore, the Mass and all its hidden mysteries are only visible to one who has given his or her life directly to Christ, awakened to their sinfulness and have approached Christ for forgiveness. Only then can we sense exactly what Christ has done for us, what our Father in heaven does in love for us, and what the Spirit will do to orient and stabilize our days. In short, only with a true understanding of our exact relationship to Christ will we come to appreciate the mysteries that lie at the heart of the Mass.

As a rule of thumb, we cannot start with the Mass to understand it, we must start with our relationship to the risen Christ in our midst. Only in Him are the hidden mysteries of the Mass fully illuminated before us.

Christ and the Church

Continuous conversion is required of us to belong to the worshiping community. Every other effort on the part of Christians to come to understand their faith, or to live out that faith comes up short. It's not even enough to belong to the Church. Apart from conversion to Christ, deep and full, even the Church is not enough. Without Christ at the center, all we see of the Church is its flaws and its failings. But in Christ, all that makes up the Church has purpose and design in God's plan. All is illuminated by the Body and Blood of Christ, when we have said yes to Him.

Look at it this way: what Moses saw in the burning bush is exactly what we are to comprehend. The bush is dry tinder, but the fire in its midst is alive. Our focus can never vary from the fire. The bush is not our focus, until we fully acknowledge the fire at its midst. Once done, the dry tinder of the bush transforms into the transcendental mysteries of goodness, truth, and beauty within us, the Church itself becoming revealed as holy and sacred.

This also requires us to make a careful examination of our sinful hearts, coming to awareness of exactly who and what we are, apart from Christ. We must assess our failures to live apart from Him, the hopelessness of being on our own in this godless world of ours. Without Christ, it is "no-go" today.

It is not rocket science to determine what is lacking in the lives of the postmodern world. That which is lacking is simply the absolute centrality of Christ in its heart. While the world will continue to spiral downward, our lives can be changed, enriched, and blessed with Christ at the center of our days.

So, what is hidden in the Mass, there for all to see, is revealed only to those who have turned their hearts to

Christ. Hollywood will never get it. Netflix won't be able to find it. The mystery of the Mass will continue to be a black box to all who fail to be converted in their hearts to the presence of Christ that stands knocking at their door. The presence of Christ is what opens our eyes to see the hidden mysteries that really are there in plain sight.

A final thought: there needs to be a deep compassion for the times in which we live. The sense of lostness and blindness in our times is a tragedy that reaches deeply into our families, our neighbors, and our culture. Things will not get better on their own. Only prayer and awareness of Christ will guide and direct us into the future. We need to know the mystery of the Mass to see the compassion and mercy of Christ and His Father for humanity today. Compassion and mercy have to guide us to transform the pain and loss from which this world now can't free itself. The world is drowning in freedom, with nothing to grab hold of.

19. The Question the World Is Afraid to Ask

> When an unclean spirit goes out of someone, it roams
> through arid regions searching for rest but, finding none,
> it says, "I shall return to my home from which I came."
> Luke 11:25

In Luke's Gospel (18:8), Jesus makes this strange statement: "But when the Son of Man comes, will he find faith on earth?" Those words are shattering. Notice that there is no response on the part of the disciples, no further questioning, no immediate recognition of what Jesus has just said. If I were a disciple with Jesus at that time, I probably wouldn't go there either. In fact, it is way too much for even now, despite the nihilism of the postmodern world.

The question that goes unasked in these times is "Who is Jesus Christ for us today?" The question cannot even be imagined, much less articulated, in such an age as ours. I have wondered again and again why this is so. Is it amnesia? Is it fear of Christ the judge? How could a world in such mortal danger not be asking such a question?

Avoiding Christ

Of course, there is the issue of our sinfulness, our will to power, our self-determination, and our entitlement that has no boundaries. Unquestionably, this self-centered character of contemporary humanity is all part of why we so avoid Christ.

Yet the issue seems different than in previous ages. That piece, coming from fallen humanity, was always there, but it never erased the very thought of God or Christ from just below the surface. Today, however, Christ and His continuing presence has been buried deeper than ever before in a world such as ours. God is not even the question today.

Christ could not seem more absent in people's awareness than He is today. We live in a virtual Christ-absent environment, and that is deeply disturbing. Our lives are just too busy, and we have too much going on to even think about who Jesus Christ might be.

In Luke 11, there is an interesting little parable, the meaning of which can only be appreciated in our times. Luke's Gospel says:

> When an unclean spirit goes out of someone, it roams through arid regions searching for rest but, finding none, it says, "I shall return to my home from which I came." But upon returning, it finds it swept clean and put in order. Then it goes and brings back seven other spirits more wicked than itself who move in and dwell there, and the last condition of that person is worse than the first.

The parable is about the emptiness of the house. It seems that the emptiness is all it takes for the evil spirits to move in. I wonder if that parable might apply, not just to a house, but also to our souls and to our times.

Perhaps what is most frightening about this little parable is the thought that emptiness is enough to draw the spirit of evil into our souls. There is something central missing, so the door is wide open. The demons are coming. Is this parable the warning for this age of the secular?

Recognizing Jesus Christ, Risen and Present

Here is a little thought experiment. In the end each of us will have to address Christ about our time here in this world, either at the end of our lives or at the judgment at the end of time. If we don't know Him now, will we even recognize Him then? Is this a fair question?

Let me frame it this way. Imagine that we have lived our lives totally ignoring the presence of Christ in our midst, pursuing the way of emptiness and self-satisfaction.

Then when we have to meet Christ at the end, will we recognize this strange man covered with the wounds of thorns, lacerations, and crucifixion, an image that doesn't in the least fit with a life devoid of suffering or sacrifice. Will we know who He is? Will we even notice Him?

Or if we have never met the risen Christ in confession of our sins, will we recognize this strange man offering to forgive our sins when we don't even think that there is any such thing as sin? When we meet Him, if this is the case, how will we recognize Him for who and what He is? We would have no need of Him! What are sins anyway?

Or if we have never reached out to the poor to find the hidden Christ dressed in rags, shoeless, unshaven and unkempt, who has been residing with them, how would we expect to recognize him when at last we meet him, given our world of comfort and luxury?

Or, having lived apart from His love, at the end, how will we break through the walls of selfishness and pride, having walked the corridors of entitlement, when we meet this nobody, manifesting nothing but humility and simplicity? If we live without humility and simplicity ourselves, how will we recognize Christ?

What Happened When He Came the First Time

You might be saying, "Of course we will recognize him, after all He is the Son of God." It might be good to remember that the people of Israel waited centuries, over a thousand years for the coming of the Messiah. They had the Scriptures, the prophets, the miracles all around them. He came and was not recognized then by so many, and was ultimately killed in the worst possible way. Many missed that coming. Will it be any different for the world in His final coming?

He was manifest in both word and deed, a miracle worker, a teacher with authority unlike anyone else, manifesting a love for the poor, the foreigner, and the sinner. If they missed Him then, will it not be possible for our world to miss Him at the end of times, that He not be whom all were expecting, that He wouldn't seem like "this."

The pharisee, the scribe, and the high priest were steeped in Moses and the prophets, how could it be that they not recognize the redeemer of the world teaching and healing in their midst?

The terrifying thing about this little thought experiment has to do with the hardness of heart of which the Scriptures speak. What happens, if we live with denial over and over throughout our lives? Do we not evolve from a cat's cradle of denial and resistance to something that thickens and thickens until nothing gets through? Our minds can create an alternate reality easily, and then we can begin to live within it, in an alternate reality constructed of illusion and self-deception. If we get far enough into it, we might see no other reality but the one that we have constructed. The ultimate would be the inverted, alternative universe of Satan.

The average sinner attempts this, but is not so hot at it. Eventually the walls cave in, and the truth comes rushing in. The addictive person requires the cooperation of all around him to nourish the illusion that it is not his fault. Eventually he too caves in out of pain and guilt, and realizes the harm that his addiction has done.

Could it be, though, that persons can get so far into self-deception that they become trapped to the point of total denial, and can never get out? I lack the answer to that question, but I think that would be the end state of hell.

What's Different in These Times

I am suggesting that the times in which we live are substantially different from any that have gone before us. Never have we had an environment that has become so blinded in their existence, free of any God, and above all, of any knowledge of the presence of the risen Christ. In the time of the Roman Empire, there was a knowledge of God, albeit imperfect. Humanity then did not define itself separate from the realm of divinity, even in the process of rebelling from it.

This kind of blindness and darkness is new in our times, in virtue of its scope. As a culture, we are where we have never been before. The time before in history has never been this successful in its denial, in its total amnesia of any presence of Christ and our Father in heaven. In such a universe of emptiness, there is no soul, no self, no truth, no morals, nothing except ourselves, and we are alone in an immense and impersonal universe. History has never been so scary.

Perhaps we could describe the secularism of our times in this way. The fish lives and swims in an environment that remains invisible to it. The water is all pervasive. Never is there a moment when its ordinary life is removed from that context. It sees no water around itself, because the water is everywhere.

So it is with the secularism of our times. No longer can the ordinary person perceive easily the existence of this totally immanent environment of secularism; it is everywhere. It is so pervasive that the emptiness seems normal. Godlessness rules. Even the seeming absence of Christ has been forgotten. That Christ has been forgotten has itself even been forgotten, doubling up on His absence, doubling up in the distance it would take to find a Savior, such as Christ.

Seeing the Secularism

In order to recognize this spirit of our times, we actually have to focus on the existence of secularism. We can only do this if we perceive carefully that something intrinsic is missing in this era, something substantial and vital to life itself. In order to recognize this perverse spirit, this inverted, alternative universe of Satan, we need to clear away the debris of the material, the waste of technology, the void of our existence. But even that may not be enough.

Perhaps it can only be seen clearly in the context of Christ. Only there does secularism's invisibility surface. Perhaps it will only take the appearance of the hidden presence of Christ to us, walking in our midst, to unravel for us the chaos of secularism.

Forms of Hiddenness Today

Perhaps we should ask about how different the hiddenness of secularism is from the hiddenness of the risen Christ. Secularism, as it has grown to the present, is almost ubiquitous, saturating the culture that we are living in. You would think that this would make secularism visible, but in fact, when it is so pervasive it becomes very difficult to recognize. It just seems normal, just ordinary, everyday American life.

This postmodern context makes it so common that it becomes difficult to recognize, or to even analyze, almost like the invisibility of the water that the fish swims in. Thus the secular has a kind of hiddenness to it, despite the strange and weird absence of meaning and purpose inherent within it, belying the emptiness and nothingness that defines it when you look very closely.

On the other hand, the essence of the life of faith, the ability to see with the eyes of faith is hidden in a completely different way. What is truly Christian in this world constantly remains unapproachable without a conversion of the heart to Christ. In short, no one is going to stumble on the Gospel of Jesus Christ when satiated with the hollow experience of the secular today. What remains unapproachable for the person caught in this way is even a speck of knowledge about who and what Christ might be for us who are His disciples.

Only when that experience of the secular starts to crumble, when clouds start to form in one's soul, when it is impossible to go on with the delusions of the secular, only then does it start to become possible that there might be another kind of life that could become visible, that is, the life in Christ in its very essence. As I see it, there are many at the edge of the hidden presence of Christ, so close they can almost touch Him, but they still don't know Him yet. Such a person comes close to being a candidate for belonging to Christ. There is yet much to hope for in our times!

The Mass, as an Intrinsic Part of Our Conversion

However, for the Catholic disciple of Christ, I believe that the most valuable substance of life alone can be found at the core of the Mass, in the Eucharist, in that moment of salvation memorialized in the Mass, in the absolute action of Christ and His Father at the nexus of our salvation. Once found in the depth of the Mass, the Catholic then becomes a radiant symbol of Christ's presence, thus able to manifest the hidden Christ for all who wish to see who it is that is at the absolute center of what it means to be Christian in this era.

The beauty and simplicity of what our Father in heaven and our Savior has done is so precious that anyone who finds it, and learns to savor it, will never let go of what it is that they have found. That beauty is most there in the Eucharist we celebrate! The one who discovers the presence of Christ in the Mass and in their heart will die to hold on to it.

Without the awareness of Christ's presence and love, the world will remain like the demon who upon returning, finds the world swept clean and put in order, but without anything there. Then it goes and brings back seven other spirits more wicked than itself who move in and dwell there, and the last condition is worse than the first.

20. At the Crossroads

"Then who can be saved?" And he said, "What is impossible for human beings is possible for God."
Luke 18:26-27

So, here we are, at the crossroads, a point I had never expected in my life as a priest. I always thought we were winning in the battle to spread the Gospel. I even thought that we could succeed, if only the Vatican and the bishops would learn public relations, explain themselves better, then we would carry the day. Not so!

The erosion continues, just like the loss of Arctic glacial ice, melting away year after year. Each generation, it seems, abandons the Catholic Faith a little bit more until we have reached the point where we are truly a minority. It looks as if we have lost.

Losing the Faith by the Inch

We're not supposed to lose, are we? After all we have the good news, the key to eternal life, the answer to it all. Yet each generation seems to hold a smaller piece of the faith than the previous one, as if stranded on a piece of ice in a river, with a foothold that shrinks and shrinks! How many generations would it take before that generation is left holding on to zero, to where there would not even be fragments of morality or Gospel values left. Another 20 years, another 40? Are we there yet?

It seems as if we have bought into precisely that which is poisonous to the growth of faith in our hearts.

We have bought into exactly that which intrinsically damages who we are and what we believe. How could we have been so naive? I believe that each of us has a priority list within ourselves, and if Christ is even on that list, it is frequently way down the line.

We have determined that this culture is not dangerous to us or to our faith. We have become convinced that if we just make a few simple modifications to our Christianity, then we will fit in much better with where this culture is going. The problem is, the few simple modifications seem to be happening over and over, from birth control, to abortion, to the disappearance or reconfiguring of marriage, to the rejection of having children, and to gender issues. It looks as if the compromises will never cease. As a result we are invested in compromises, distractions, and contradictions to what we need to be disciples of Jesus Christ in the 21st century. We are losing the faith by the inch, and often cannot even see it happening.

In point of fact, perhaps it was the social gospel that influenced us, thinking that we were going to succeed in bringing peace and justice to the present times. We are supposed to be winning, right? Why are we not seeing the victory? Why do the forces of evil appear to be occupying more and more of what should be our turf? Despite all the evidence of erosion of faith in our times, we somehow naively expected to see progress in our culture, not loss of ground or deterioration of human values. Not defeat!

The Cross Is the True Pathway

Then I begin to reflect on the cross of Jesus, how that cross was victory in defeat, how Christ lost everything in His efforts to bring the new creation into existence.

When I start to reflect on this reality, I begin to realize that I have gotten myself stuck somewhere between Good Friday and Easter Sunday. Holy Saturday had to have been the darkest day in history, as anyone with even a thread of faith and hope was lost that day, defeated and destroyed by what had happened, Christ, the hope, murdered in the most vile of ways.

I once saw a sculpture of Joseph of Arimathea, carrying the dead body of Jesus to the tomb that he provided for Jesus' burial. You could feel in the sculpture that it was all over, gone, that all that hope of the disciples was now useless. This was perhaps what the two on the road to Emmaus were talking about when the risen Christ began to walk and talk with them.

Why should we expect anything else in these times other than the cross of Christ, the same kind of defeat, the same kind of darkness that deluded Satan into thinking that he had won. The cross has been and always will be the gateway to the resurrection. Why wouldn't it be that at the final coming? Instead of looking for success in human terms, instead of looking for progress in current history, we are to embrace the journey of the cross in our times.

Perhaps there was a time when we thought that we could ratchet up peace and justice, so that the world would have no choice but to join with us. Perhaps that is what led us into assumptions that the world might be evolving into the kingdom of heaven, and that victory was just around the corner, a kind of incremental eschatology! It would have been easy to assume that the fight for justice and peace was something we were to bring about here and now.

The Coming of Christ

But then if Good Friday was the secret to the resurrection, why would not the cross be the secret to the final coming.

Also, what will fortify us for the rest of the journey in our times is the Mass and Eucharist. If the Mass encapsulates the moment of victory on the cross, then the Mass will perfectly position us for the moment of victory yet to come in the crisis of the cross in our times.

We know that the Last Supper and the crucifixion are intrinsically connected, one single event. So too, the final coming might also be so connected as one event, gathered in timelessness to the cross, to the Last Supper, and to the celebration of the Eucharist.

The defeat that we already feel in our bones in this world is simply the backside of the victory to come. Each time we reach the depths of the Mass and the Eucharist, we stand at the threshold of the final mystery, a mystery that has always been there for us from the moment of the death of Jesus, a moment that is encapsulated in the celebration of the Eucharist, a moment where time stands on end. The coming of Christ was in Israel, is in the Eucharist, and will be in the end of time. It is all one and the same!

21. Nothingness and Death

> Learn a lesson from the fig tree. When its branch
> becomes tender and sprouts leaves, you know that
> summer is near. In the same way, when you see all these
> things, know that he is near, at the gates.
> Matthew 24:32-33

There is a question in philosophy that is often said to be the most basic question you can ask. The question is, "Why is there something rather than nothing?" Supposedly, you can't find a more basic question that this.

However, in the 21st century the question for the secular world might be reversed: "Why is there nothing rather than something?" This second question has no satisfactory answer, and is, frankly, frightening to ask.

Even in a culture centered on nothingness, "something-ness" keeps popping up, and can't quite be scrubbed from deep within the soul, annoyingly asserting itself, just when desire seems to have gotten rid of the troublesome temptation to find truth.

When we have detached our minds from God, and our souls from Jesus Christ, we are simply left with nothing, an annoying and discomforting contradiction to what resides in our hearts. This nothing is so prevalent today, that it seems to have substance, a weight, ending in a resultant dissatisfaction.

This nothing of our era takes up a lot of space, and it is the only certainty of a world without the Father and the Son. Where there is nothing, there is no salvation, no redemption, no forgiveness, no hope, not even right or wrong. There is nothing to account for, no purpose, no destiny, no source, no point, just nothing. This is the breathtaking abyss of meaning for today's world.

Faith Seeping through the Nothingness

Nothingness is big today, in a new way. Faith has always managed to seep through to the soul of people, calling them to turn to what is above, what is from God the Father. The nothingness of this era removes the possibility of finding your way to a God above. Our planet looks more and more lonely in the universe. This beautiful blue orb where we live is seemingly connected then to nothing. And it looks as if we might be in danger of losing even that with our rapidly shifting climate, and our obstinate ways as creatures of this planet. This blue planet seems the only thing that we still have, and we are losing that, inch by inch.

Death takes on, in this context, a massive weight. It is the unavoidable and the undefinable, to be delayed through every effort possible. Death in the postmodern world must be denied in order to cope.

It has been said that our struggles with health insurance are really about an irrational fear of death, trying to make every effort to avoid dying, trying to immunize ourselves against the day, when even what little we have will be no more.

One wonders if the crisis in health insurance that this culture is going through isn't directly related to a disbelief of an afterlife or a God. Medicine seems to have an almost irrefutable obligation to preserve life no matter how expensive and complicated that decision might require. "I have to go on living, no matter what, and it's an entitlement."

Over the years of my ministry I have had ample opportunity to witness the difference between someone who looks at death as a simple doorway and someone else who looks at death as a collapse into the final abyss of nothingness. In the first instance, death is a sacred and beautiful moment, in the second, an absolute disaster.

The Crushing Reality of Nothingness

The absence of any God or any afterlife, in the postmodern world, goes a long way to inflating death to unusual proportions. If this world and this time is all there is, the human being has no other option other than to hold on to living as best he can, seeking every way possible to sustain and protect what he has here and now. A secondary loss for the postmodern world is that any and all morality ranks behind this need for survival, as if to say, my life is more important than right and wrong, justice and peace. My needs rule!

In addition, there is no freedom in a world of absolute freedom, when you can lose it instantaneously at the moment of death. If freedom becomes absolute, as it would seem to do in the realm of the secular, then in freedom all is allowed. Then, the more freedom there is, the more likely it turns to a form of slavery, controlling everything else in one's life.

It is both striking and breathtaking that life could be defined without there being anything other than this minimal nothingness. If so, this is a crushing reality. How does one operate in such a vacuum?

If you've bought this package, and you look up, there is nothing above you. If you look below, also nothing.

In the end, even looking horizontally at this life, then there is also nothing. No wonder, in contradiction of contradictions, suicides continue to multiply in this era. No wonder, then, there is the escape of the drug culture, in a twisted sort of logic, an escape from death and its minions, often leading to death itself. No wonder that sex becomes the only thing left to the secular world. No wonder freedom becomes an unbearable abyss of choice.

Orphans of the Universe

Here's another thought experiment about the victims trapped in the secular. Given a climate of nothingness, absent anything of substance to hold on to in this 21st century, humanity is reduced to being an orphan of the universe. In the midst of millions of galaxies, billions of stars, and probably even more planets, here sits much of humanity, orphaned by its own agnosticism, having long forgotten that there might be someone, a Creator who is the source of all that exists — to which they might actually turn to and to whom they might belong.

In our world, the orphan has always had to struggle doubly to find his or her identity, without the presence of parents, left free-floating, unconnected to family, having to make their own way in this world. Eventually, the orphan overcomes his or her isolation, and finds a new family or surrogate adults in their lives to help put together an identity, as it were, to start the beginnings of a whole and complete life.

However, imagine the challenge for the orphans of the universe, with no connections to anything, all alone, isolated in this failing blue orb of the earth, in a seemingly endless and purposeless universe. Could they be any smaller than to be alone and orphans in such a universe? Could there be any more tragic and hopeless orphans than owners of this postmodern world? Being orphaned in this way would make death even more chaotic and inexplicable.

The antithesis to the orphans of the universe, however, are those in the world who understand that the entire purpose of the universe, that the center of all creation are the children of God, and the disciples of Christ. We come to an awareness in our prayer and understanding that we are the capstone of all that has been created, and the point of the incarnation and redemption. We are the reason everything we know and see exists! We know that:

> He chose us in him, before the foundation of the world, to be holy and without blemish before him. In love he destined us for adoption to himself through Jesus Christ. (Ephesians 1:4)

All the millions of galaxies and billions of stars, and everything else, is pointed to our existence as temples of the Holy Spirit, that our existence is the completion of purpose and design of the universe, all of it, centered and focused around the dying and rising of our Lord, Jesus Christ, dictated and directed by the love of the Father. Even our deaths end up being the final step into eternal life in Christ, death itself ending up flush with purpose and meaning!

Death for Disciples of Christ

In the Catholic funeral liturgy we pray at one point, at the final commendation: "Father, turn toward us and listen to our prayer. Open the gates of paradise to your servant."

Our confidence in God hearing our prayer at that moment is breathtaking, a virtual command to God in our pleading! At this point the liturgy is crystal clear, there is a future. Even our deaths are purposeful. Death ends up a doorway, not a wall. It is not an ending, but another beginning.

And we know this is so, because during our lives we have witnessed the continuing love of Christ for us in the Eucharist, the coming of the Spirit all those times when we needed divine help. God has at various times spoken to us about forgiveness of sins, reconciliation with our brothers and sisters, and the Holy Spirit has guided us with a spirit of hope that has never left us.

Every celebration of the Mass breathes of a new reality about life and death. In the moment immortalized in the Eucharist we see the death of Jesus cutting a doorway into eternity, coupled with an embrace on the part of the Father to all who are connected to Christ. This understanding removes the contradiction of nothingness, the death that dogs this postmodern era and the orphans of the universe.

I doubt that there is anything much more traumatic than to lose a child. I once had a woman, who was a pediatric nurse, come and ask to become Catholic. When asked why, she simply said that she was the witness to many deaths among children in pediatrics, a leading hospital in that field, and that she noticed something about the parents who had just lost a child. She said she sensed something different in those who were Catholic, that they had some inner resources to fall back on at such a time. She said that she wanted that resource for herself, lest anything happen with her and her three young sons.

Our Catholicism is a Eucharistic reservoir of strength and support. Even in our sins, we are not at a distance from Christ. He stands there waiting for us, shoring us up in our needs, even when we are lost and can't find Him.

All this should turn us toward our postmodern world, with a sense of compassion, and a ready, if unspoken invitation, to become a part of the treasures that Christ has laid out for us in His moment on the cross.

Those treasures are explicit in the celebration of the Mass. The better we know these treasures, the more our invitation will become spoken. The hope of the postmodern world will be in coming to know Jesus Christ, and His love for us. And that is made clear in the depth of the Mass. Once we truly grasp what is intrinsic in the Mass, our lives will radiate and illuminate the presence of Christ for our times.

The Moment of Communion

One of the aspects of the Eucharist, intrinsic to our dealing with this strange new world of the 21st century, is that in each celebration of the Mass we have the act of receiving Christ into our hearts, both in the celebration of the Word and in the reception of the Eucharist. This act, both on the part of Christ and on our part, is an act of renewal of our fundamental decision to make Jesus Christ the center of our life, in the conversion of our hearts to Jesus Christ.

Often you see in televangelists that there is an altar call, inviting attendees to come forward and declare themselves for Jesus Christ. I respect that action a great deal.

However, it is only one moment, not ritualized or repeated. Only in the Mass do we make that decision again and again, giving Christ the opportunity to touch, deepen, and strengthen the commitment that we seek to maintain. In the Eucharist we declare again and again the Amen of Christ's presence with us, and our own recognition that He is the center of our being.

What a different pathway we are led down, with Christ at our center. How different from the nothingness of our times. How disarming to the power of death. The lordship of Christ in our hearts saturates us with new meaning, holds us in place, and commissions us with His Spirit.

The further these times try to lead us into a world without God or without the presence of Jesus Christ, the more terrifying the nothingness of our era will become, the more frightening the future. The more we, on the other hand, center ourselves around the presence of the risen Christ, as He is manifested in the Eucharist, the more we are able to stand at peace in such a world.

A Bit of Gratitude to the Secular

Curiously, I find that there is truly a value to the secular for us in our Catholicism. Nothing but this context of secularism could more clearly focus for us the inherent, astounding worth of the Blood of the Chalice. The more the secular dominates our culture, the more clearly we can see this secularism as an empty container, plastic and cracked in its very nature, not enough to build even a partially complete life around.

The absence of anything redemptive, anything uplifting, anything credible in the secular, can only lead the faithful Catholic to a deeper and deeper grasp of Christ's love and the Father's love for us. The more the nothingness of our times, the chaos of life in this valueless system, the more the quiet, peace-filled character of the presence of the living Christ will radiate in our midst and in our hearts.

Perhaps, then, we will need to be grateful for what this secularism reveals to us, warns us of, and punctuates what we have, leaving us breathless with joy at what we carry in our hearts about the love of Christ in these strange days of the postmodern world. Nothing could possibly awaken us more deeply than this strange milieu regarding the absolute gift of being a part of the new creation, and being given new life in Christ.

How marvelously the Gospel works, using even its opposite to highlight and illuminate this miraculous new life within us. The more secularism becomes dominant in our times, the more the good news of Jesus Christ will touch us. Even Satan's inverted, alternative universe becomes a vane pointing back to the Gospel, for those who love Christ.

In addition, the better we understand the central moment of the Mass, the more deeply we participate in that central moment, then, the more clarity we can have about what it is that creeps around and tries to assault the doors and windows of the places where we celebrate the Eucharist.

So, either way leads us to the truth, amazingly. If we look with clarity toward the secular around us, the presence of Christ will astound us with its nearness. If we look with clarity toward the sacred character of the Mass, the emptiness and hollowness of the secular immediately becomes evident, and quickly moves us deeper in union with the presence of Christ in our midst.

In the end, as we reflect on this milieu in which we live, and identify its hollow character, the pathway to holiness and salvation will be even more illuminated. Thus, even the secular points us to Christ. Hence, we could have even a bit of gratitude to the secular in which we live! Even that is a mirror reflecting the Glory of God!

22. What Has Changed?

> Jesus then said to the Twelve, "Do you also want to leave?" Simon Peter answered him, "Master, to whom shall we go? You have the words of eternal life. We have come to believe and are convinced that you are the Holy One of God."
> John 6:67-69

There is a story that comes from the Orient. It seemed that a village was split over a major issue in the village. Everyone was at everyone else's throat. The village leaders scarcely knew what to do, so they invited Confucius to come to the village to solve the dispute.

Confucius came, and the villagers waited to see what he was going to do. However, true to his nature, he surprised them. He simply sat down in the middle of the village, oriented to the west, doing nothing.

As the villagers awaited some action by Confucius, they gradually realized that all he was doing was orienting himself to the four directions, and that what they need to do regarding the problem was to orient their minds and hearts to a sense of order, and they could solve the problem of the village themselves.

We are in a similar situation today. The chaos of a godless culture has ripped apart the roots of morality and ethics today. Purpose and destiny, identity, and our connections with the past have faded like a mist of fog. The media points in every which direction. There is no guide in these times, none that people can find as long as there is no connection to faith in Jesus Christ. There are answers galore, none that work, save one.

I have been a priest for over fifty years now, having lived in this period of transformation as radical as the Reformation, both in Catholicism and in American culture. That timespan bridges the last days of the immigrant American Church right up to the present situation.

The Breakdown of Generations

The heart of what I have watched and experienced is that faith frequently fails to pass from one generation to the next, except with great focus and effort. Today's Catholic grandparents often wonder what they did wrong that their children grew up only to abandon their faith. In fact, they did nothing wrong, the bizarre growth of the culture simply pulled the rug out from under them.

In the 1950s there was a kind of ghetto Catholicism that thought that Protestantism was the enemy. It was not. With the Catholic schools, the religious congregations that served in the schools, and the abundance of clergy, Catholics existed in a microcosm, semi-independent of the rest of American life. It was safe, because it was hidden from the culture of that time.

To this day, when I visit the cemetery where my family is buried, I recognize all the names of those of the Catholic parishes and community where I grew up. It was that close knit. Even the cemetery was segregated from the Protestant cemetery. Catholic life was a tight, self-controlled environment, in many ways separate from American culture, where it seemed easier to maintain your Catholicism from one generation to the next.

After that time it became increasingly difficult to pass the faith on to the next generation. Despite our best efforts, we continuously lost out to the climate of secularism and to the agnosticism of the times, to the media, to the wealth that defines modern life, to the subculture of adolescence, to the Internet and the cell phone, and to the instability of marriage and the family. In the end, we Catholics have become a minority.

Through the last part of the 20th century, we witnessed again and again the futility of our efforts to withstand this change, and watched parents, broken hearted by the abandonment of faith of their children. Vocations declined. Parishes lost population. Schools closed.

Often, when families returned for the funerals of their parents in the parishes they grew up in, now only one or two of the seven or eight children would still know how to participate in a Mass. The others no longer remembered when to sit or stand, sometimes bringing water or soda to the Mass as something to drink, as if holding their breath to endure this time in church.

After the hundred years of the 20th century, we now know that if marriage and family are not supremely oriented to faith in Jesus Christ, the faith link between generations is lost. Parishes also have to be Spirit filled both in liturgy and ministry for that continuity to connect. Clearly, it is possible to pass the faith forward to the next generation, but there can be no inattentiveness to the faith life of the family and the parish. Catholicism cannot be a low priority; it must be number one on every family's list of priorities today, or it will not endure. There are no shortcuts to faith today.

A Radically Different Future Required

The essence of the problem is that we have to find a new way to pass the faith onward. The things we depended upon before the Second Vatican Council no longer worked. I believe that the times in which we live now are closely akin to the beginning days of the Church, when everyone had to be evangelized in order to bring them into the light of Christ. There was nobody, no Christians before them in the Empire. Those first Christians had to start from scratch, possessing only the message they had heard regarding the Good News of Jesus Christ.

When they heard it, they realized they could step away from the paganism, the sexual exploitation, the slavery of the Empire. That message was transformative for them, so much so that they were willing to die for what they had gained. They had found something astounding. Now their lives had purpose and meaning. They discovered what love actually was, as demonstrated by the Father in the sending of His Son, and in the self-sacrifice of the Son out of love for humanity. That message rippled through the nations and through the generations.

We have to do the same now. I understand how radical this is, compared to how we tried to live before in this culture. Everyone in the family has to be evangelized and fortified to the maximum degree in order to hold on to their faith in Jesus Christ.

We are now missionary territory. Several generations have experienced these breakdowns of faith. Our culture now is more and more peopled by those who were baptized, but now live as if no church or faith was necessary anymore. At times now in this culture we, who are still Catholic, end up feeling like fugitives, having to seek out others like ourselves with whom to share what it is we value, but have to keep hidden from still others.

This situation may actually be to our advantage if we can learn how to evangelize from scratch. A culture that has evolved in such a fashion will bring many opportunities to bring people home to Christ.

We first need to understand the context in which people are trying to survive without Christ in their lives. The postmodern world with which people are faced today is in many ways a failing patchwork, pockmarked with gaps, ultimately unsatisfying in its outcomes, an environment laced with sexual fatigue, drowning in freedom.

We need to exploit the emptiness of secularism, the cost of excessive freedom, the onus of entitlement that undermines the lives of those without an awareness of Christ today. We need to identify what the results are of attempting to live without God, or without the presence of Jesus Christ in these times. Why the opioid epidemic? Why the suicide rate? Why the failure of marriage in this culture? Why the chaos in ethics today?

The Spirit in Our Midst

Also we need to notice the signs of the Holy Spirit in our days. Why the increase of vocations that is quietly occurring? Why all the grassroots efforts to begin new ministries in parishes that we find? We need to understand what is happening below the radar in parish life, and in Catholic families. There are many signs of hope for the faith.

The more secular the culture becomes, the more opportunities we will have, as individual souls awaken to the emptiness and disfunction of the secular way of life. Such a way of life is characterized by the loss of truth, the absence of beauty, the trampling of goodness and the evaporation of any intrinsic meaning to life today.

Our way of life in Christ is characterized by these transcendentals, lifting us upward toward the call of the Gospel. Even the evil of our times points the way back to Christ for those who have lost their way or been ensnared by the illusions of the times. Anyone with an open heart will be invariably drawn to conversion toward Jesus Christ.

Our faith must start with compassion for the lost sheep of the 21st century. If we have made Christ the center of our lives, the first priority in our lives, we will then be drawn close to those who are trying, with much difficulty, to live without Christ. The secular age is homeless, when the only home possible is in Christ.

Self-Examination

In order to do this, we need to understand our own sins. We need to refocus our baptisms. We need to know deep down that it is only Christ who can complete our lives and enrich our existence. We need to know exactly what Jesus Christ has done for us, from where we have come, what the presence of Christ has changed in our own journey of faith. We need to know the identity within us that can only come from a deep commitment to Christ.

In the present age, all are missioners and evangelizers. Often we find this a scary challenge, as we don't know how to do what the Spirit seems to be asking us to do. However, all we need do is find a new, deeper level of commitment to Christ, and to the level celebrated in the central moment of the Eucharist.

Finally, we have to find the way to orient ourselves in the right ways, to see clearly, to understand what is happening around us in this culture, and to comprehend our nature and tendencies as human beings.

Fundamentally we need to be converted from the ways of the culture into the Body of Christ. This can only happen today for us who are Catholic through the aid of the Mass. The Mass is the hidden resource, the starting point of all these challenges.

Let me put it this way. The Mass, the Eucharist, lies at the heart of what we are to become in the 21st century. We all carry the effects of Adam's sin, the tangled judgment of will over intellect. The good we hope for on our own simply breaks down and becomes tangled up in what is worst in us. We lose our orientation, especially in a culture that no longer recognizes that there is a God who has created us, or who keeps us in existence, heartbeat by heartbeat. We now live in the midst of a culture that thinks that Jesus Christ was simply a good man, murdered 2000 years ago.

The Mass as Gyroscopic

As a child, my father once gave me a gyroscope. It consisted of a spinning top within a metal framework that allowed the top to find its own equilibrium. The amazing thing was, that in your hand, if you changed the hand's orientation, the gyroscope pushed back against your hand, as if seeking to keep its original orientation. The gyroscope seemed to protect against the pitch and yaw of the hand's movement.

A gyroscope brings orientation and direction to many things that this world has created. It is truly a wonder of the age. Every air flight we take depends on gyroscopes, even our cell phones, I think, contain one. They are ubiquitous.

The Mass acts as a kind of gyroscope. In the Mass, we come in direct contact with Jesus Christ. His presence, His word, His Body and Blood push back against the tendencies of our fallen nature and against the vertigo of the world in which we live. As we enter more and more into the Person of Christ, the more powerfully Christ orients us to navigating this world in these times.

The deepest way to orient ourselves in this generation is by our total understanding and fidelity to the Mass. Nothing else can orient us today as well. Prayer helps, the Bible enriches, the Divine Office supports, Adoration strengthens, almsgiving adds, love of the poor has to be there, but it is the Mass that is the secret, hidden, fundamental and foundational source of treasure in our Catholicism, continually reorienting our souls, providing balance and direction to our weakened and flawed human nature.

The Right Place, at the Right Time

In the act of receiving Communion, we usually think only of Christ coming into our soul. What we should also recognize is that we are taken into Christ Himself. In that context, we become a part of Christ, thus changing who and what we are. Christ gives us the orientation we are incapable of on our own. Christ balances our sense of direction.

Jesus Christ alone gives us true purpose and promises a real destiny. He brings us back when we wander away. He lights up for us who we are to become, the only path that makes sense in terms of our humanity. In Christ, we know who we are and why we are living.

The Mass, if we enter into it deeply enough, will provide us protection against the confusion of this postmodern secular society. The presence of Christ in our hearts, fostered and deepened by the Eucharist, is precisely what we need to be the missioners and evangelizers of our times, not necessarily by words, but by the radiance of His presence in our hearts. The Eucharist is also exactly what we need to strengthen our marriages and families.

In effect, as the saying goes, we now have got the world right where we want it, Satan exactly identified as never before, the truth available as never before either!

In some sense the postmodern world is Christ's moment. The conversions will come. Anyone who has bought into this world today, staring at himself in a mirror in these times, can't help but be saddened by the state of the soul of the one on the other side of the mirror. Those alone, without God or Christ in our times, can feel the panic rise up in their heart. Christ will be there waiting, knocking at the door, waiting to share a meal with us. Strangely, sin, failure, and even evil will bring people to Christ.

We are in the right place at the right time. All we need is the orientation that the risen Christ in the Eucharist can give us. Never underestimate the Holy Spirit!

23. Goodness

"God saw that it was good."
There is a question that, as a priest, people will
often ask. It is this: "Am I a good person?"

I never know where to go with that question. Usually the person asking is looking in the wrong place. They are looking inside themselves, at their sins and failures. Perhaps the place to look to appreciate their goodness is in Christ and in what His Father in heaven has done, and in what the cross has done for the person asking the question.

For certain, the only one who can answer that question is our Father in heaven, or His Son, Jesus Christ. What goodness within us seemingly has two sources. The first is God Himself. In our creation He has placed a spirit of goodness deep in our souls, that awaits there for our conversion, the waters of baptism, and the coming of the Holy Spirit. The second, of course, is an awareness of what the dying and rising of Christ is about, with regard to our very selves. Thus, it would seem that Christ and His Father have already answered this question about whether we are good persons or not.

Perhaps, when people are asking about their goodness, the question is actually about whether their sins will outweigh any goodness that God has placed within them or that Christ has done for them by dying on the cross.

This is troublesome territory for us. We wonder if what we have done wrong might possibly eviscerate any goodness that might have been placed within us.

Can our sins destroy whatever goodness God has placed there? Can our sins be greater than what Christ did on the cross? Can forgiveness and mercy ever be less than Christ's action on the cross?

At root, we might suspect that somehow our sinful actions will make our salvation impossible. This, of course, is one of Satan's central arguments.

The Awakening within Us

The fact is, God is not satisfied just to place goodness within us, but sends His Son to arouse the final awakening to that goodness in our hearts. There is a part to our goodness that hides within us, only to emerge at the knowledge of what Christ has done for us, where we truly discover Christ's love, despite our sinfulness and our failures. Our Father in heaven has never ceased to pursue us, to bring us home, to surprise us with what mystery we are, to discover deep within us what He has placed there. This knowledge only emerges from our union with His Son.

The Sacred Scriptures tell this two-part story. It begins in the creation narrative of Genesis. Six times in the days of creation it ends with the statement: "God saw that it was good." This is a tip off for us that all of creation in God's plan will center around goodness somehow, especially within our very hearts. God has put His spark within us, breathed His spirit in us, buried His treasures deeply within us.

However it is only in the New Testament, in the words and deeds of Jesus, that we come to understand the extent to which our heavenly Father and His Son are willing to go, to reveal for us what it is that we are to become, and to what extreme God will go to unwrap the goodness that lies deep within us.

The Goodness in the Gospels

In the Gospel of Luke, Jesus, whom we refer to as the Good Shepherd, goes out from the ninety-nine to find the lost one. It is an illustration of how far Jesus was willing to go to bring us home to the Father. Little does it show at that moment in the Gospel just how far Jesus was willing to go to accomplish that; He will go all the way to the cross itself.

> What man among you having a hundred sheep and losing one of them would not leave the ninety-nine in the desert and go after the lost one until he finds it? And when he does find it, he sets it on his shoulders with great joy and, upon his arrival home, he calls together his friends and neighbors and says to them, "Rejoice with me because I have found my lost sheep." (Luke 15:4ff)

Then there is the scene in the parable of the prodigal son, where the father seems to be on the lookout for the return of his son so that he might welcome him back. The father appears to have never given up that the son would return, that his return and celebration afterward would prove the worth of the son, despite the son's failure.

> So he got up and went back to his father. While he was still a long way off, his father caught sight of him, and was filled with compassion. He ran to his son, embraced him and kissed him. His son said to him, "Father, I have sinned against heaven and against you; I no longer deserve to be called your son."

> But his father ordered his servants, "Quickly
> bring the finest robe and put it on him; put a
> ring on his finger and sandals on his feet. Take
> the fattened calf and slaughter it. Then let us
> celebrate with a feast, because this son of mine
> was dead, and has come to life again; he was
> lost, and has been found." (Luke 15:20-24)

Then too there is the parable of the lost coin, no doubt, of a woman living on the edge of poverty, badly needing that coin to make ends meet for the sake of her family. When she finds it she hosts a celebration. The coin speaks deeply to us of our worth to the Lord, that how we who were lost proved to be somehow deeply valuable to the Father and the Son.

> What woman having ten coins and losing one
> would not light a lamp and sweep the house,
> searching carefully until she finds it?
>
> And when she does find it, she calls together her
> friends and neighbors and says to them, "Rejoice
> with me because I have found the coin that I
> lost." In just the same way, I tell you, there will
> be rejoicing among the angels of God over one
> sinner who repents. (Luke 15:8-10)

Perhaps the most telling of parables is that of the buried treasure and the pearl of great price. When I was younger, I assumed that we were to be the ones who were supposed to search for the treasure or the pearl. I assumed further that these things were representative of finding the good news of Christ and giving up what we had in order to obtain it.

> The kingdom of heaven is like a treasure buried
> in a field, which a person finds and hides again,

and out of joy goes and sells all that he has and buys that field.

Again, the kingdom of heaven is like a merchant searching for fine pearls. When he finds a pearl of great price, he goes and sells all that he has and buys it. (Matthew 13:44-46)

Only later did I reevaluate the point of these two little parables. Suppose that it is not we who are searching for the treasure or the pearl, but rather that it is God Himself, our Father in heaven, who is searching for the treasure and the pearl, that it is the Father willing to sell His Son in order to purchase these things.

If that becomes the meaning of the parable, then the parable seems to be saying that we ourselves are the treasure, we ourselves are the pearl of great price, and it is the Father who searches.

If we give the parables this interpretation, then they seem to define our value, our worth to the Father in heaven. This also highlights the passion and love our Father in heaven has toward us, the love which propels Him to sacrifice His Son, and the willingness of the Son to go to the worst possible point of humanity in order to bring us to the point of goodness.

What God Sees in Us

Of course these two simple parables make sense. After all, we are God's creation, the creation summed up by the words: "God saw that it was good." I suspect that God is much less interested, and not in the least focused just on our sins. The Father is much more focused rather on the fact that He wishes us to be with Him in all eternity, that He has invested Himself in the flawed and corruptible humanity that we have become, trusting in the possibility that we who have been created might then become the treasure He originally intended for us to be.

All of this takes on its definitive meaning in the cross of Christ, that the very purpose of Christ's sacrifice was to bring about in us a new humanity, one that the Father had planted deeply within us from all eternity, but was hidden away behind the sin and selfishness of our lives. The cross of Christ reveals to us the extent to which God was willing to go to bring about this new creation.

All the way through these examples and parables is the message from the Lord, that God intends us to be precious and holy, that our lives are sacred, brimming with meaning, rich in the makeup of our essence. Naturally this makes sense. God could not create anything that was not good, or at least destined to become good. Goodness is one of the primary traits of our God, if not the one most high in God. Beyond that is the effort of our God to bring this about within us, creation climaxing in redemption.

The Mass Radiates Goodness

All of this then radiates through the liturgy of the Mass. We constantly have the experience of being surprised that God could love us to this extent. We all know our weaknesses and our failures. How could it be that God would find something of worth deep within us? How could it be that we receive the Body and Blood of Christ deep within our hearts? What is God trying to say to us throughout the Mass, from the Scriptures to the Communion. It comes as a great surprise that the Father had no other intention in sending His Son but to save us. Christ could have had no other intention in dying than that we would be made worthy of the grace and mercy flowing from that event.

Quite possibly the hardest thing in all of our faith is the knowledge that God loves us with an unending love, irrespective of our character. This mystery lies in a realm far beyond our comprehension. No wonder we are repeatedly taken to that very moment in the Mass when the love of the Father and the Son around the cross is pinned to our consciousness, is imprinted deep within our hearts, and leaves us astounded at what has happened to us as a result. We can never fully grasp what it is that our God has done for us, has intended for us, or has loved in us through this creation and redemption. And, in the Mass, we are repeatedly brought to that central moment.

24. Without Christ, with Christ

> Jesus went around to all the towns and villages, teaching in their synagogues, proclaiming the gospel of the kingdom, and curing every disease and illness. At the sight of the crowds, his heart was moved with pity for them because they were troubled and abandoned, like sheep without a shepherd.
> Matthew 9:35-36

When I was younger, I often enjoyed three-dimensional puzzles. These puzzles often looked like a sphere or a cube when put together. Almost always there was one piece to the puzzle that was the key to the whole thing. Without that key piece, none of the other pieces would stay together, and the whole would collapse into a pile of sticks or components. Once you found the key, and inserted it into the pieces, the whole thing would stay together and the puzzle would be complete, stable, and looking almost like a piece of art.

These puzzles are similar to what it is like to attempt to put our life together in this postmodern world. In fact the postmodern world looks to me like a search for a missing piece that simply does not exist in our secular world, that could have completed a life, defined a self, or fulfilled a destiny for someone living in these times.

In William Golding's novel, *Lord of the Flies*, after everything has collapsed for the children and they are gathered around the hog's head, "the Lord of the Flies," the head speaks, saying that it is the reason it is "no-go," the reason all ended in failure. Such is the case today, the one thing that the postmodern world needs is the one thing they can't find. They seem to be trying everything else, and it is no-go. Beelzebub is not the answer.

The Times in Which We Live

These times are not like any that have gone before. This world is more and more clearly a lost world, hopelessly committed to doing its own thing. Every real connection with what has gone before has been severed, both philosophically and theologically. All is now free floating, relative, and undefinable.

In this context we are confronted with climate change which will require a total rethinking of how we are to live together, and we are paralyzed by even the thought of it. Heroin and opioids each year are claiming more and more lives in a hopeless spiral of dependency, taking mostly the lives of the young. We have no idea what to do about it. Marriage is fragmenting, the family broken, morality without an anchor. Even the young can feel it; they lack the self-assurance and confidence in the future that youth used to have in the last quarter of the twentieth century.

In the 19th century, those times found a way to get rid of God. God was first redefined as distant, and then, ultimately, as dead. The God that they assassinated was not God, but a concept of Him, something they could limit, and thus dispose of, something silent and disinterested.

Thus they redefined everything in relation, not to God in heaven, our Father, but in relation to themselves, who then had the power to be whatever they wanted to be, because the God of the past was gone. So, as it were, in secularism we were now god ourselves. We finally held the secret to freedom and fulfillment. Nothing could stop us.

However, the one piece, necessary to complete the puzzle of life, is still present to those who know where to find Him. The missing piece is the risen Christ, hidden at the threshold of any heart that is open to Him. He is the one who brings things into focus. All it takes is conversion of heart to Him. He then is that missing piece that brings the loose ends of our lives into a harmony, one that doesn't fix our world, but orients the disciple to an inward balance, and an understanding of where we have come from, why we are here, and where we are going.

Identity becomes indefinable without this essential piece in our lives. When I know the presence of Christ in my heart, destiny and purpose stay. That presence receives its confirmation and reinforcement in the Eucharist. Our endurance flows freely from the experience of the Christ present in the Mass. Once we place the risen Christ at our center, all falls into place spiritually.

The Presence of Christ for our Times

Jesus Christ is not so easily disposable as the 19th century God was. Losing God was an opportunity for the self to emerge, victorious and self-sufficient. The superman had arrived, upon the exit of God.

Surprisingly, the question of the presence of Christ is a lot more troublesome then God was. God was silent, Christ has a voice. He speaks through the Scriptures, and through the Church. He touches people. He keeps arriving, when at last you thought you were free of Him. He shows up in our minds, our hearts, in current events, in the poor, in the suffering. He refuses to stay back in the first century. The cross and Golgotha reaches right into the 21st century, the third millennium.

The reason Jesus is so troublesome is that He came as one of us, at the very crossroads of divinity and humanity. He died on the cross for our sins, and will come again to judge the living and the dead. Each of these things get underneath the systematic denial and pretense, under the skin of the desperate secularist. Try as our world might, they can't push Him back to Jerusalem two thousand years ago.

We know that denial takes a lot more energy than acceptance. Lying to self requires a whole network, a whole constellation of intent to maintain. That we are accountable cannot be scrubbed out of our nature. And if we are accountable for what we do, that means we are accountable to someone. That someone is not a 19th century god, but to Jesus Christ, Lord and Master of the universe that is here now, and is coming at the end of things, the same one who died for us on the cross.

The Keystone

Here is another image that might help us to understand the extent to which Christ has gone to draw us into His new creation. That image is the one of the Roman arch. Across the Roman Empire the Romans built aqueducts, bridges, and buildings, using the simple architectural form of the arch, whereby the entire arch was held in place with a keystone at the top of the arch. Once that keystone was in place, all of the stones in the arch were locked into place. If the keystone was removed, the rest of the stones simply fell into a pile on the ground, useless and without purpose.

That keystone is an apt symbol of what Jesus Christ has done for us. When we discover His presence and His love, the pieces of our lives have an order, and can support all the dimensions of our lives. To discover Christ is the heart of our salvation, without which we would struggle on the edge of chaos. In Christ, each of us has our place, each of our lives take on a meaning, every part of our day ends up having significance for who we are and what we are becoming. In the end, in Christ, we become a kind of architecture, made whole and complete with Christ as our keystone.

Sheep without a Shepherd

There is a sadness in our times, in this postmodern existence, simply because of the nature of life without Christ. Existence today for many is simply like the image of a pile of rocks that lacks a keystone. These times of a secular world amount to existence without any unifying principle, without a personal presence that would dignify and consecrate life.

Where Christ is absent, there is no keystone. Without Christ, existence is just a pile of rocks, undignified, random, and purposeless, an attempt at community without the only one who has the power to unify our communities. What Christ saw long ago, in His ministry to the people of Israel, is especially acute today: "At the sight of the crowds, his heart was moved with pity for them because they were troubled and abandoned, like sheep without a shepherd" (Matthew 9:36).

Our heart needs to go out to those in our world today. Never has the world tried to live such lives, with Christ's presence somehow undiscovered. There needs to be a readiness on our part to share the joy and peace of knowing Christ in our hearts, so that this world might desire to discover what it is within us that has such a source of goodness and completeness, one that this world cannot find on their own. This world needs to be able to see that there is something within us, that there is a mystery that defines who and what we are, that anyone without Christ would want to find, in the midst of living in this pile of rocks to which secularism reduces this world.

Thus the significance of the Mass for this age of secularism. We orient ourselves to Christ again and again within the mysteries of the Mass. Once we take ahold of Christ, present to us when He is offering Himself totally to His Father in exchange for our salvation, we begin to take on the fruits of the Spirit in our everyday lives, our souls radiating beyond ourselves the spirit of joy and peace that the lost ones of our times can see and thus be drawn to.

Part of our experience at Mass must be an awareness of where souls today struggle with the emptiness of existence. The sadness of our times belongs in every celebration in the Eucharist, right along with the depth and the beauty of the mysteries of the Mass. The joy of having found Christ for ourselves has its counterpoint in our awareness of how souls suffer in these bleak and forlorn times apart of the one person, Jesus Christ, whom they need, but can't yet find.

The Story of a Man in a Tree

There was this rich man, dressed to the nines, wearing a three-piece suit for his day, gold cuff links, silk tie, and a set of three hundred dollar designer shoes. Everybody around him knew his way of becoming rich was dishonest, yet they were still jealous. He had status, even if he was somewhat short.

There was one more thing. He was up in a tree, of all places, for some reason, up in a sycamore tree. Nobody of his status would be up in a tree. People up in trees are anything but important, usually just foolish. His name was Zacchaeus.

It was there that Jesus found him, saying, "Zacchaeus, come down quickly for today I must stay at your house." I suspect that there was a wry smile on the face of Jesus at the humor of this situation. How could Jesus have kept a straight face at that moment! Anyone who thinks there is no humor in the Gospel should look closely at the incongruity of this situation.

Why would someone so wealthy and important be so interested in seeing Jesus of Nazareth, unless there was something going on inside this man, willing to go up a tree to see Him. In addition, I wonder how far out of the way Jesus had to go to find this man, and I wonder even more what it was that Jesus saw in him that made Him go looking for him.

> Jesus came to Jericho and intended to pass
> through the town. When he reached the place,
> Jesus looked up and said to him, "Zacchaeus,
> come down quickly, for today I must stay at
> your house." (Luke 19:1-5)

I believe that this little narrative encapsulates the very essence of what happens between a person and Christ today, when Christ is finally encountered. In essence the heart of the matter is that Christ goes in search of the person in need. This is a narrative repeated over and over within the Gospel. We need to understand that this encounter is still occurring. The astounding thing is that Christ says that He is coming to Zacchaeus' house today.

Later, the Book of Apocalypse will echo this moment:

> Look, I am standing at the door, knocking. If one
> of you hears me calling and opens the door, I
> will come in to share his meal, side by side with
> him. (3:21-22)

Then there is the one in the tree, Zacchaeus, seeking to see the Christ. It is done in all sorts of ways in our times too, a chance encounter with someone of faith, a crisis where all the answers of the past no longer work, or an accidental visit to a Mass or a church. Any of a thousand ways the hidden presence of Christ reveals Himself. Yet, how common was it and is it that Christ said that He wants to share a meal?

An Archetype of the Eucharist in Every Encounter

In some sense this encounter of Zacchaeus and Christ is an archetype of the conversion experience. In this era it is easy to begin to think that nobody has any interest in finding Christ today. Yet there are thousands of testimonies every Easter Vigil about how someone was searching for Christ and was found by Christ at a critical point in their life. While our secular era keeps repeating that no one has any need of Christ, the encounters continue today! Often the encounter is a surprise beyond all expectations, so much so that at first the person doubts that it is happening to them, or that it simply isn't real.

That encounter often leads to baptism, and to falling in love with Christ in the Eucharist. Note carefully how often Jesus comes and shares a meal with someone, and how they knew Him in the breaking of the bread. One almost senses an archetype of the Mass throughout the narratives of the Gospel.

We must raise our expectations today. Christianity is not over. In fact, I would suggest that there is an inverse proportion at work here. The more Christ is scrubbed from our times, the more He is forgotten, the less someone knows about Him, then, the more likely that person will meet the risen Christ at some point in their life. I can't give you a proof of this in any scientific format. I only know that the risen Christ lives, and there is nothing else that makes sense in our age.

I think it a reasonable expectation that Christ, the Good Shepherd; Christ, the one seen from the tree; Christ, the one next to the thief on the cross; Christ, the one Nicodemus comes to in the night — that He will come to anyone in this era who has an open heart, that yearns for something that makes sense in these times.

The Approaching Harvest

Only for that purpose was the Son sent into this world to die on the cross. The more this world becomes devoid of Christ in their awareness, the closer He will come. The less the world is aware of Christ, the more likely they will find Him if their heart is open. The time of the harvest draws near.

I often think that when I see or read of an avowed atheist so enraged or dismissive of faith, I personally believe that the more he protests, the closer the call of Christ is to that person. That person is then truly in danger of meeting the risen Christ in person.

Witness Cardinal John Henry Newman, living in the 19th century, deciding to write a book about how Catholicism was in error, only to find himself in the process of being converted to precisely that Church he sought to condemn. The closer Christ comes, the more stressful the denial becomes. Look at Paul and his 180 degree turn on the road to Damascus. No conversion since has equaled that turnabout.

This postmodern age is not the time of the defeat of Christianity, rather it is the first steps of the age of the harvest, the coming moment of victory as seen in the journey to the cross. The more Christ is ignored, the more the world struggles to deny Him, the closer He is to being recognized.

In the end, you cannot deny Christ without an acknowledgement that He is. Christ is the Lord of history, the judge of the world, the one who is coming. And the world knows it, deep in its heart.

25. The Eventual Meeting with Christ

> Some of the Pharisees who were with him heard this and said to him, "Surely we are not also blind, are we?" Jesus said to them, "If you were blind, you would have no sin; but now you are saying, 'We see,' so your sin remains."
> John 9:40-41

Sometime back there was a comic strip called "B.C.," projecting human events humorously back, as if in the time of cavemen. One particular character had found some reference that said that the human body was 98% water. Whether it was based on any fact was irrelevant. This particular person went through life avoiding thinking about that possibility, and avoiding where possible any reference to water. When confronted with that situation, he would withdraw into a kind of panic state, until he could distract himself. However, the reality was always there in his mind. That he was 98% water, so he thought, undermined all the rest of his life. He just couldn't get away from it. There was water everywhere.

People say the same about spiders. We shouldn't be afraid of spiders, as at no point in our lives are we more than three feet from a spider. I suspect that is an exaggeration, but this analogy works too.

The fact is that the risen Christ is omnipresent in our world today, but also totally ignored. I believe that the presence of Christ is the one reality that can't be faced in the postmodern world. Clearly He is a danger to anyone who would deny Him.

Easier Now, Than at the End

Let's put it in these terms: the meeting up with Christ at some point, either now or at the end of things, would be profoundly frightening to anyone who chooses to deny Him in everyday life. The final coming of Christ is the ultimate moment of meeting or confrontation. Christ is the Lord of life, the judge who is to come. This is the reality that can't be looked at for those in denial.

For the modern world, steeped as it is in denial, it is not death that will be the big problem, it is the inescapable suspicion that after death we shall have to meet the Lord of life, for real, in truth.

This meeting is bigger than death, and overshadows death deep in our hearts. The meeting of the risen Christ, the King of the universe, simply can't be looked at in these times. That meeting, when it happens, will invalidate the denial we may have made throughout our life, those choices that assumed that I could do anything I wanted with my life, because this material world was all that there was.

The agnostic world, that most have chosen to live in, is a construct, a house of cards, flimsily built, unstable in its essence. Just one moment of having met the risen Christ is enough for that entire world view to be shattered. Even the thought of such a possibility would need to be suppressed, as it would invalidate everything that the postmodern world presumes.

Here is how the collapse takes place. There is a Christ, living and present to our existence, and so there will surely follow a day of judgment by the Lord of life.

If that is true, why have I not found Him before? Why have I not acknowledged Him? Have I needed to deny His existence, so that I am free to choose my own pursuits, my own entitlements? And how could I possibly come to know Christ, if my whole existence is based on making myself the center of the world? Christ alone can be the center of all creation, including the center of my life. If my life is totally untrammeled and unlimited by anything but my own ego, can I stand before him? As the "B.C." character thought, what if I am 98% water?

The tendency of the modern world is toward a kind of thoughtless agnosticism, a form of rather careless denial about the realities of divinity that form the bedrock of human existence. This form of thinking has proceeded without much attention to where we have come from, why we are here, or where we are headed. In addition, this attitude is reinforced in this world where there is not allowed any mention of God's existence, or of the presence of the living, risen Christ.

What I see is a world basically drifting aimlessly without much attention to what might be hidden within and behind our existence. In most cases, this kind of aimlessness is unintended or accidental, but nonetheless, devastating. However, it becomes a threshold of fears, causing the individual to question his or her assumptions. What if I dare not look at the presence of the risen Christ in our times, and then have to meet Him at the end of things?

The grip that the world holds in this kind of thoughtless agnosticism tends to be shaky. This generation sits on a slippery slope where there is to be no mention of anything that comes from above, from the Lord of life, or anything that comes at the end of things. Anchoring oneself in this kind of a world only works as long as you not look too carefully at your own existence. What if I am 98% water?

The Supremacy of Human Will, Today

The point is, given our nature, intelligence, and consciences, the human person tends clearly and honestly toward the truth both about our divine origin as well as about our redemption in Christ. The obstacle in this truthfulness usually comes back to the fact that Christ's presence won't line up with my own will, in my being at the center of my own life, in the willful choices that I want here and now.

The real assumption that this generation seems to be making is that the truth lies in material things, and that the spiritual is nonexistent. I believe it is quite the opposite. We are beings straddling the line between the material and the spiritual, and between the two there is no contest.

We have come from the Lord, from above, and Christ is alive as the redeemer and Lord of our lives. The material piece of our lives gets us nowhere. There is no content to the material, but a plethora of content in the spiritual.

I heard a story one time of a man on his hands and knees, searching for something on the ground under a lamp post. Another person came up and asked what he was looking for. The first man responded that he had lost his car keys. The second said, "I will help you look."

After a while the second man said, "Are you sure you lost it here?" The first man replied, "Actually, I lost it over there in the dark somewhere, but this is where the light is. So I thought I would look here."

Modern man thinks that he is in the light, that it is where you can see with your eyes that you should look. Actually, only with the given eyes of faith can we find what it is that we need or seek. The risen Christ in our world, a hidden but real presence, is simply the truth of reality. Not to accept that presence in our midst is an aberration. If He is present now, He will surely be revealed totally and finally at the time of His final coming.

The truth of Christ is that He is indeed coming. His return in the final days is absolute. This truth in normative, despite whatever denials our world tries to make. The world's reduction of all reality to only what is material is the height of denial, and is an attempt to escape our spiritual nature.

So here we have this great spiritual mansion that God has given us. Why would anyone choose to live in the potato cellar of materialism?

The absolute starting point is that we have come from above, from the Lord, and that we are always in the light of God's love, manifested through the cross of Christ, celebrated day by day in the Eucharist.

26. There Is No Other

> Turning and turning in the widening gyre
> The falcon cannot hear the falconer;
> Things fall apart; the centre cannot hold.
> "The Second Coming,"
> by William Butler Yeats

It's funny how we are drawn to things that frighten us: rats and spiders, wild animals and creaking doors, lights that flicker inexplicably, all accompanied by gravelly, murmuring music. Then there is another whole section of things we are scared by: ghosts and demons, the walking dead and zombies of all sorts, malevolent forms of evil, blobs, insects, even sharks falling from the sky.

When I was a kid I remember seeing the film, *Forbidden Planet*, a film at the vanguard of science fiction and horror movies. That film focused on evil monsters that arose from within a person's dreams, and came to destroy the dreamer, hence that planet was a forbidden zone. What fun it was, and how scary, the monsters jumping right off the screen, right at you!

Then, too, there is an underlying fear that the contemporary world holds today, strange preoccupations in science. Will the caldera at Yellowstone suddenly explode again soon? What if another asteroid crashes into the Yucatan just like the one that destroyed the dinosaurs? It is almost as if the more we understand the science of our planet, the more there is to be frightened of. It could all easily end for our planet someday.

The Irrational Fear of Christ

The Pharisees found something to be frightened of also. They were frightened, terrified by Jesus! How could it have been that this humble, truthful, and gentle man could have been so frightening to them, so too, to the scribes and the Sadducees. Even the high priest was afraid.

Jesus carried no weapons. He had no political party. His followers were nothing more than fishermen, and there were not many of them. Yet the Pharisees and others needed to rid themselves of Him, eliminate Him, supposedly for the good of the people, but really just for themselves. They found Him terribly frightening,

It wasn't the last time either. The Romans found Christ a threat also. They could no longer get to the Christ, as He had become the risen Christ, hidden and invisible to those without faith. As a result they focused on His disciples, usually the poor, the marginalized, slaves, and commoners. Now they too became scary just like their master. But make no mistake, it was really Christ that was the underlying source of all their fears! What could it have been that made this one so frightening?

Even more, this same irrational fear has happened throughout the history of the past 2000 years. Whenever the poor or the marginalized were awakened to the presence of Christ, they became frightful to those who were in power.

Missioners entered a culture, and people there quickly began to convert to being disciples of Christ, almost as if they had been waiting for the announcement of the Good News of Jesus Christ for centuries. Almost always those in control were frightened by this event. At times there were thousands who were martyred. It took the Roman Empire two hundred and fifty years to stop creating martyrs. What was it that could have been so frightening about the powerless, the poor, and the marginalized?

When I came to work as a missioner in Korea, one of the older Maryknoll missioners there, Fr. Mike Zuno, told me, that when he was sent to a village, shortly after the Korean war, "I couldn't believe that a people could be so good and not yet know Jesus." Clearly, they had no fear. But in the 100 years before that time, the ruling class there martyred over 10,000 of the Korean people. There are similar stories in Vietnam and Japan, in Latin America, wherever the Gospel was preached.

The root of all of this fear is a single person, Jesus Christ. On the surface, it was the poor and broken who had become His disciples, but at root, it was always Christ that the powerful sought to destroy. It has been Him and Him alone of whom they were so frightened. Of course, they could not get at the one who was responsible, as He is now hidden and invisible to those without the eyes of faith, so they persecuted His followers. In culture after culture, these new disciples of Christ became martyrs for Christ, but always the target has been Christ Himself.

He was the problem! He was in the beginning, He is now!

Today, the one the world is most frightened of is the Lord Jesus Christ, the King, the judge of the world. Make no mistake, He is the one to be destroyed. The world is frightened to death of Jesus Christ. The risen Christ lives at the center of humility and poverty, a fountain of love to all around Him, a source of renewal and redemption, in the midst of a fragmenting and self-destructing world, determined never to let go of their climate of entitlement.

Needing to Destroy Christ Today

The present time is the time that is the most interesting in all of history. Here in the 21st century, the forces of the world think they have now succeeded. Instead of trying to murder the source of life within us, they have taken new steps to obliterate the very existence of Christ from consciousness. As a result, seldom do you hear anything about Christ from the media. Christ appears absent from film, television, contemporary events, absolutely everything today.

No problem seems to be solved today by turning to Christ, to opening hearts to Him and inviting Him in. He is long gone from consciousness of the average citizen in daily life. If there is a reference to Him, it is that He only lived thirty-three years about 2000 years ago, the implication being that there is nothing relevant about Him for today. He is history. He is gone. No more, nada, nothing, irrelevant. Not just forgotten, but they have forgotten even that they have forgotten, dubbed over, as it were. Thus the fear beneath everything, seemingly buried along with Christ.

This is a new form of murder, a step beyond crucifixion, done in a form that the high priest and Pharisees could only have looked on with eyes of jealousy, His elimination from consciousness and awareness now having been so thorough.

The Source of the World's Fear

There is an explanation for this, however. I believe that these total efforts to eradicate Christ today are the result of the increasing and evolving fear about the inevitable coming of Christ. The time draws nearer for the coming of the King of the universe.

Deep within the hearts of humanity, there is a fundamental knowledge that Jesus Christ is coming again, and the time draws nearer and nearer. This truth is fundamental, and is lodged in the deepest resources of the human soul. This truth is inescapable, and the nearer it comes, the greater the fear of that day, the deeper the attempt to bury it.

The times we live in are actually a time of monumental fear about Christ, far beyond that of the fear of the Pharisees, scribes, and the high priest. Thus the need of total denial, of an absolute erasing of the least trace of the divinity and humanity that is joined in Jesus Christ, now risen and alive.

Hence the need for the total absence of awareness that there ever was a Savior in this world, that He mattered more than anything else that happened, or that He is risen and alive and in our midst today because He defeated the power of Satan by means of His dying on the cross. The closer it comes, the greater the fear, the more the denial.

I mentioned above about the world's preoccupation with natural disasters that could end the existence of the human race, the asteroid suddenly descending from space, the nuclear disaster waiting to happen, the exploding caldera. These potential events take death to the power of ten, ending not only individuals but all of history, all of art, all of knowledge, and an end to the blue pearl of the solar system, the earth.

I suspect this is God's final warning to us. In addition, it is a final proof that this collective existence, this creation is not eternal, and that its loss would simply be beyond comprehension. It would be a moment of condemnation beyond all condemnation for humanity. All of the story of creation coalesces here into an ultimate tragedy.

The Unanswered Question

There is a classical musical piece, by Charles Ives, the American composer, called, "The Unanswered Question." It is short, about seven or eight minutes in length. In it, there is a background of strings, representing the universe's endless existence. In front of that background, there is a single trumpet, that repeats a simple melody, reminiscent of a question being asked. The question is never defined, only restated musically again and again.

Seven times it is repeated. Six times there is a response by several orchestral pieces, attempting to answer the question, each time growing more and more dissonant and chaotic, the sixth time, void of any harmony. The seventh time, there is no response but silence, and it's over!

The sadness that musical piece conveys is beyond imagining, fear being turned to absolute grief. A feeling that we have squandered that blue pearl of the solar system, possibly even of the whole universe, having betrayed our God and our Savior Jesus Christ.

Yet, in the midst of these times, here we are, Catholics, gathered in prayer and worship around the presence of Christ in our midst, around the central moment of the cross in the celebration of the Mass. Could there be any greater contrast than this contemporary world that has a willful amnesia about Christ, and we who center ourselves completely around the presence of Christ in the Mass and Eucharist?

The Mass today exists as an isolated island in a turbulent sea of egoism and secularism. The Mass today, in its quiet and ignored existence, survives as a moment of beauty and truth, constantly being lifted up in the love of Christ, in the presence of the Holy Spirit, and in the ever watchful eye of the Father.

In the forgetting of Jesus Christ in these times, even our existence as disciples of Christ becomes forgotten and hidden to the world, misidentified as some superstition or fantasy.

In the chaotic times of today, we go on, below the radar, centering ourselves thoughtfully and intentionally on the Christ who is our peace and joy, to whom we belong, in whom we are fully at home in hope.

The hiddenness of this reality is astounding in the midst of such secularism. Once again, like a diamond in a bed of gravel!

Thus, on one side there is a world with an undiagnosed fear that Christ is coming soon, and on the other side there are assemblies of believers, keenly aware of the presence of the Christ that the world has suppressed from its own memory or awareness. It is the nonexistent Christ of secularism versus the overwhelming moment of our salvation in Christ celebrated in the Eucharist. Could the contrast be any greater than this?

The Root of All Fear

My belief is that the fears that the postmodern world likes to play around with—belief in the presence of demons and ghosts, of the power of Satan, of the weapons of evil and violence, even nuclear war—is simply a way of masking precisely the more fundamental fear that there is a Christ who is coming soon, and that all the efforts to scrub His existence and His coming from consciousness simply don't work.

This fear is not irrational, rather it is the most logical of fears, built around the truth of the Word of God. It is not evil that is frightening, it is goodness and love, that if this world has rejected it, it will come eventually to condemn it.

Further, it is not God primarily that frightens these times. After all, the world declared God dead long ago. My belief is that God was declared dead for the sake of escaping Jesus Christ, because it is specifically Jesus Christ who is coming soon as judge and King of this world.

I think it might be a little easier to run away from God than to run away from Christ who alone is the mediator, the one who was incarnate, walked among us, died and was raised from the dead.

Friedrich Nietzsche, the 19th century philosopher, who first declared God is dead, missed the mark. Christ is clearly the danger to this world, above and beyond anything else. He was the one sent, from above. What could be more scary than a humble, gentle person with the power to forgive and to reign over all?

In the end everyone will be confronted with the acceptance or rejection of Christ. He is the way to the Father. The choice is specific to Jesus Christ. To think that we will have to meet Jesus Christ, and have to choose or reject Him is the literal heart of fear in our times. In short, His coming is definitive, final, the absolute limit to things as they are today. No more stalling or delaying, it will be over, and we will each have to choose, Christ or another. And there is no other!

Often the portrayal of Satan is common today. His image appears acceptable in the media or in film. He is portrayed as a creature of power, some alternative to pursue for gain in this life. Frequently, Satan seems the only power in our world, Christ, of course, being supposedly nonexistent and absent, the result of the postmodern world's amnesia.

Thus, violence is the new sacrament, according to Satan. It is supposedly the only way things are to get done. The death penalty is his eucharist, scapegoating his instrument of renewal, all of it done to delay the day when it will be totally revealed that there is none other than Christ.

The Antidote to Fear

That central moment in the Mass, when we celebrate the moment when Christ gives everything of Himself to the Father, and the Father simultaneously accepts that sacrifice—that moment symbolically suggests the final coming of the Lord into our midst. Thus here we are celebrating exactly what the world is afraid might happen. In that moment in the Mass, we are there with the Father and the Son, at peace and speechless, rapt in attention, while all around us the world continues to flee that confrontation, suppressing it in every way possible.

How fortunate we are when we focus our faith around the sacrifice of the Mass, and the key moment of our union with Christ and His Father. This act removes us from the source of fear and leads us deeper and deeper into the gift of the love of God for us, manifested in His hidden, real presence with us. The Mass is the antidote for our age; it is everything the world is not.

Satan has no place here, he is simply unnecessary and irrelevant. The gentleness and love of the risen Christ governs all things for those who give their hearts to Him in the Mass and the Eucharist. In the Mass there is no other but Jesus Christ and His Father, and the love between them: the Holy Spirit. And of course, you and me!

Naturally we have our fears, but they come from our weaknesses, but in the midst of those fears, we have the knowledge, the truth of the One who gave His life, totally and completely, that we might live in a new way, and that we might sense the love and dignity that Christ continuously showers upon us. Most certainly, we know that our union in Christ binds us beyond all fear to our Father in heaven. There is no other.

27. Analogies for Our Times

*When he disembarked and saw the vast crowd,
his heart was moved with pity for them, for they
were like sheep without a shepherd.*
Matthew 9:36

A long time ago I used to watch the evening news. However as I grew older, I noticed the commercials were all directed to illnesses and conditions of aging, trying to market medicines to those who are older. That was depressing, since I too am aging. In addition, the news each night turned out to be less than the sum of its parts, almost always disappointing to me.

One time, before I gave up on the evening news, I caught one of those little snippets that the news would end with, almost always a human interest story introduced to gloss over the bad news that would form the content of the day. One time, the news commentator cited something that happened at one of the "big-box" stores, somewhere in the Southern U.S. It seems that they had opened a new store, and it had sliding glass entry doors that would open and close automatically for the customers.

The curious thing is that there was a flock of swallows that somehow learned to hover in front of the door and the door would open for them as well, and it opened both from the outside and from the inside. Once the swallows had learned this, they proceeded to make the store rafters a great place to build their nests. The store was getting as much traffic at the front doors from the swallows as it did from the customers. So it was that these birds were able to use the same technology as the customers, and thus had a safe place, heated and secure, up in the rafters to raise their young, free of predators.

Automatic Doors

I don't know how this little story came out in the end. The news report never said. However, that image of the swallows going in and out through the sliding doors amounts to a wonderful image of our times. The swallows knew nothing of the electronics that enabled them to open and close the sliding doors. They had no knowledge of the math that was behind such a technology. They didn't know how the doors opened and closed. They didn't even know why those doors did what they did. They didn't know where the store came from, or why it was there or even how it was built. They just knew that if they hovered in the right place, they could enter.

How similar to us in our times. Those questions that the swallows didn't ask, much of our world today doesn't ask about their existence. We often know nothing of the mystery of our existence, of how our body is marvelous beyond imagining, about how our human progression happened, that we were lifted above the animal level. We miss the incredible complexity and symmetry of our very own DNA. We fail to think about this strange universe, with its millions of stars and galaxies. We traverse our days without thinking about where we have come from, or why we are here. We don't know our origin or our destiny. We are often as unknowing and without a sense of perception, just as this flock of swallows was.

To boot, we often live without a theology, not understanding our broken and wounded nature that undermines our existence. We are scarcely aware of what it means that God sent His Son that we might be lifted up. We don't perceive the power of the cross, and how it changes things for us. We fail to note the living presence of Christ in our midst. Finally, we don't even begin to fathom the mystery of the Mass, and the difference that it can make in our existence.

This is what the postmodern world can do to us, taking us away into an apparent comfortable existence in these times, as if there were nothing behind all of the world in which we live. We become like those swallows, uncomprehending, ignorant about most of what this life is about. We don't need to think about where we have come from, why we are here, or where we are going. Everything opens up automatically, so we think. Why do we live like those birds, uncomprehending, oblivious, taking it all for granted?

Looking for a Box to Hide In

Consider it in these terms: if you have ever had a cat in your home, and you brought in a cardboard box for them, you know that the cat will crawl into the box and curl up. It is particularly cute when the box is small, a shoe box or something similar. The cat will just about perfectly fit inside, all curled up. Why do cats do that? What is it that they like about that experience?

I actually have no idea why cats do that, but I think it can give us an analogy for our times. The technology of today, the length of our lifespan, the wealth of contemporary America seems to give us something that we can wrap around ourselves, almost like what the box does for the cat. It seems secure, even when it is not. In these times, we have the illusion of security for a time briefly, and we don't have to think about those pesky, difficult "why" questions. We can avoid the origin and destiny puzzles. There is a belief that we are somehow living in the best of times, that we need not think about the poverty in our souls, or that all this is to come crashing down upon us at some point, and that we will have none of the tools necessary to cope with or to survive what might happen. We're quite like the cat in a box.

Amnesia, Required for a Secular Existence

No age has ever been like this age. It is catastrophe in the making. What this contemporary world seems is no more than that cardboard box that the cat loves so much. These times require a kind of functional amnesia in order to maintain the massive spirit of denial about our existence. Even when God is labeled dead, He just won't go away, He is always just around the corner, and our cardboard boxes are just not enough to keep Him away. The risen Christ is here, radiating compassion for us, but is invisible to anything but the eyes of faith, so close that you can almost feel His breath. Instead, we hide from Him, wrapping ourselves in anything we can find. Like a cat in a box! Why do we do that?

How vulnerable the present age is. The denial of our nature, the lifestyle that we are hiding behind, the ego that we are so busy branding and protecting, all of it is not enough to cover the reality of what we are, where we came from, and why we are here. The wall that the modern world hides behind is thin as cigarette paper, nothing more than a leaky membrane, where the truth persistently seeps into empty souls.

Awaiting the Harvest

We are on the fringe of a time of evangelization. There's no question about what is coming, or what any thoughtful and sincere human being needs today. There is no question that it is only in Christ that anyone in this era can find an authentic peace and sense of meaning.

We are to ready ourselves for those who will awaken and come to us, seeking the very Christ that we possess. If anything, the coming days are not days that will be bleak or hollow for the disciple of Christ, but will rather be a time of enlightenment from above about who our Father in heaven is, where to find His Son, and what it is that will make us whole and complete, even in the midst of this era of fragmentation and illusion.

When I was privileged to work as an associate missioner in Korea with the Maryknoll Missioners, I witnessed the widespread growth of converts to the Catholic Church there. At one of the parishes I served in, Tandedong Catholic Church in Seongnam City, South Korea, we would put up a banner at the gateway of the church, inviting new members to the parish. Again and again we would do that, each time gathering thirty to forty new catechumens seeking to be baptized and catechized in what it meant to be Catholic. This occurred several times each year, bringing new members into the faith. At times, at Sunday Mass, about 20 to 30 percent of the attendance would be those who were there for the first time, seeking to enquire about how to become Catholic.

When I would return to my diocese here in the U.S., the priests would ask how could that be happening, as nothing like that was happening here in this country. The only answer I could give, as to why, was that it was the harvest in that culture. After suffering Japanese occupation for 40 years, enduring the Korean War, and having to rebuild from total poverty, it opened the hearts of people to the presence of Christ that they now knew they needed in such an unstable and chaotic era in their country. It was the harvest there and then. In the end, it was Christ who had manifested Himself in their midst. And, they got it!

It is not yet the harvest here in the U.S. However, that time will come. Now is the time of planting in this culture. For certain, the harvest will come. There is nothing that can satisfy the hearts of our culture short of the presence of the risen Christ in our midst. Everything else is either illusion or subterfuge. Everything else is Satan's inverted, alternative universe.

I don't believe that most of those, who are caught up in where our culture is taking them, are truly advocates for the agnosticism of the postmodern world. Rather, I think, they have been caught unawares of the pathway they are taking, that they are kind of comfortable, much like the cat in the box. Our hearts need to stay with this generation, as much of the promise offered to this generation is pretense, of the sort that only a 21st century politician could insinuate, with very little leading to justice, fairness, or truth.

We prepare our hearts now for the coming of that day when it will be the harvest. As always, the heart of that preparation starts and ends with our participation in the depth of the Mass, in the centering of our lives around the central moment of the cross, celebrated in every Mass. Only in the Mass can the richness of the presence of Christ and the love of the Father be found in total, preparing us to receive the souls that will be the harvest of faith that is to come.

The Context of our Times

Context is everything in this generation, and much of the context today is this secular environment in which we have to live, whether it seems deceptively like we are swallows before automatic doors, or cats in boxes.

There has never been a time like this in the past, not in ancient Jerusalem, not in ancient Rome, not in the Middle Ages, even in more recent times. This secular age is new, and mostly invisible to us as a time.

We are like fish swimming in the ocean, who cannot even imagine their existence without water. This context in which we live has all the dimensions of an absolute emptiness, a context devoid of any symbols or pointers to the spiritual, transcendental life that Christ has invited us into by means of His dying and rising. This context is both subtly frightening by itself, but compelling us toward the Blood of the Chalice. Such is the situation we face today.

We need to understand what people are experiencing in this time of ours, divorced from the presence of Christ in their lives. Never has there existed such a desert of meaninglessness, but never has the presence of the risen Christ been more appropriate. The loss of identity and meaning cries out for Christ to come to show the way.

The struggle of our culture to hold together and to maintain itself, given the emptiness and chaos of our secular times, can potentially turn many to the knowledge of Christ's presence in their lives. This is almost a perfect environment for the Good News of Jesus to spread. These times cry out for Jesus Christ to be present for anyone with an open heart.

We need to have immense compassion for people living in this age. Secularism is an empty castle, and many caught in it will await an unknown redeemer, for sure.

Once we understand that, the words of the Gospel will well up within us. While on the surface, people appear fulfilled and satisfied with the wealth of their lives, just below the surface lives a kind of loss and ennui that contradicts what shows on the surface. Many yearn for something spiritual and transcendental, but can't find what it is that will bring peace. They need the presence of Jesus Christ in their hearts and their lives, and our compassion for them will help them draw closer.

It is in this context that the Mass has a great role to play to orient us in these times. If anything is a contrast to this age of nihilism, it is the Mass. The Mass rolls up together in itself parts of beauty, silence, and the presence of the risen Christ, the absolute antithesis of this empty world of the 21st century within which we have to live.

There is a peace in the Mass that is different from the peace that people think they want. This peace exists in the celebration of the Mass and flows from the cross itself. This peace is the presence of Christ, offering Himself to the Father, totally and completely, in perfect humility, poverty, and obedience. It exists nowhere more in the universe than here in the Eucharist. The Mass orders our lives, and orients us around the exact center of things, the Christ who is with us. Fundamentally, the spirituality of the Mass can completely focus us in addressing the context of these times and the emptiness of this agnostic age.

28. On the Importance of Our Sins

> Perhaps for a good person one might
> even find courage to die.
> Romans 5:7

This amazing moment of redemption, of being born again in Christ is almost beyond comprehension. This moment between the Son and the Father happens in the context of our sinfulness. We weren't deserving. It shouldn't have happened that we were found. Everything about our desires and actions should have put us beyond the pale of salvation. There was no logic, humanly speaking, about what Christ did on the cross, or how His Father in heaven responded, certainly not from our end.

What the Father has done, for the one who repents, is that He looks right past our sins, passes them by and goes right to the good that He had planted in our hearts from even before our creation. It is not that God doesn't notice our sins, but that His focus is beyond the sins, toward all the good that He intends to bring out of us. The interest of our God is not toward our sin, but toward our redemption. I almost see it as a kind of studied, purposeful aversion on God's part regarding our sins. He simply leaves us to the darkness when we choose to turn from Him, in a kind of preview of what hell would be like.

However our Father in heaven never loses focus on what He desires for us. His creative plan from the beginning of time is clear: hide within us all that could be good, then find it again in the new creation, when we have said yes to His call.

This new life is the supernatural within us, that Christ's death and the Father's acceptance brings out of us. We had no idea that gift was there within us. That's part of the monumental surprise of the Good News. That's what stunned the first Christians. That's what stuns anyone today who has found themselves having been grasped by the hand of Christ, and pulled into a form of life that they, who at the very least, had not suspected could ever have happened, or who had found themselves lifted up into something they had originally denied or opposed. It was all there from the beginning, and we just didn't see it.

The Strange Role of Our Sins in Our Salvation

It's not that we are to overlook or forget our sins in our quest of the divine life. Quite the contrary. Nothing can bring us to understand the dimensions of our redemption than to realize that all this has taken place within us over against our repeated failures to transform our lives, that again and again we have been inadequate to the task of reform, that we have been blind to the truth and the beauty of God's love.

This work on the part of Christ and His Father has not resulted from anything within us other than our painful declarations that mercy and grace has been given us. Humanly speaking, this mystery did not deserve to happen. Maybe somewhere there are people who were deserving, but I am not one of them!

Our sins are useful, even after many years. Our sins bring into focus the extent to which Christ went on the cross, enduring alone the darkness and isolation of His suffering and death. Our sins open our minds to what the measure of the Father's love really is. That measure, frankly, exceeds our ability to comprehend.

I think we will never get to the level of understanding what God has done in our lives, or to what level God has loved us. We will never get our arms around it! The reason our past sins are so useful to us, is that our sins magnify the dimensions of God's love in our lives. Those sins should have been an impassable abyss for us, isolating us forever from what we were intended to be. Instead, Christ's love found a way through, a bridge over them, handing us to the Father as an imperishable gift to Him. How incredibly small we are, yet how much worth we seem to be to the Father. How the Eucharist celebrates all this!

The Escape from Sin

Our secular world has found the way around all of this. Sin is simply eliminated. All is permissible. Not only that, I as a human being have a right to do whatever I want, or to take whatever I think I need. "I am entitled." Nothing is allowed to disturb the liberty that the modern world thinks it so badly needs. As a result, the mystery of God's love goes undiscovered. This absence, this denial of the mystery of God's love requires an accountability with regard to sinfulness. Apart from that accountability, what's left? Only the empty container of secularism filled with only echoes of hedonism and greed, and a hunger for meaning that can't be satisfied.

We are strangers and foreigners to this contemporary culture, not at home here, more than any other generation. Yet we are the possessors of the divine in the Eucharist. We have a home; this world is just no longer it. We celebrate an unseen but true reality, one we have been invited into by the love of Christ, by the exact instant when all of history is reconciled by the cross of Christ, celebrated in the moment of the Eucharist. At that moment we are indeed home. We who had no access to the divine by ourselves have been taken in by the love of God for us.

The truth is, in the parable of the Good Shepherd, there are no ninety-nine sheep, we are all the one whom the Good Shepherd has found. We are the ones invited to the wedding feast, found without a wedding garment until the waters of baptism, yet somehow, by the time it is over, are lifted up into this feast, made worthy, made acceptable in an astoundingly altered course of events.

And the sins that captured us in our past—they made it all the more unlikely, but it is all the more remarkable that, despite those sins, we have been caught up in such mystery. And in each celebration of the Mass, we are somehow brought to this very moment of the transformation of all of our humanity in Christ's sacrifice of the cross. We somehow have ended up, somehow brought to an impossible moment that should not be, humanly speaking, yet nonetheless is.

29. Hearing the Voice from Beyond

Jesus said to them, "I am the bread of life; whoever comes to me will never hunger, and whoever believes in me will never thirst."
John 6:35

Hollywood and television are located in a strange place, struggling to portray faith and Christianity, while not quite knowing what to make of it, clueless as to what it is truly about. In addition, in what I believe is an effort to not overly define faith or church, you see Hollywood take kind of an eclectic approach, blending elements of Catholicism with Protestantism, smearing together both the Mass and the worship of the Protestant churches, in an effort to make things seem acceptable to whomever happens to be watching the television. Often they confuse faith with a sort of magic. There will be vigil lights, Catholic vestments of a traditional nature seemingly out of the early 20th century, alongside of the stained-glass windows that could only come from the Protestant tradition of the Good Shepherd—all of it vaguely suggesting some sort of ecumenical watered-down Christianity that really doesn't exist anywhere other than in Hollywood or in a television series.

Once in a while, however, they get it right. There was a series called *Hell on Wheels*, about the building of the transcontinental railroad in the 19th century. There was a character, called Bohannan, who was the main character throughout the series. As always, this character was a mixture of good and evil, whose life was a series of misadventures, leaving behind a trail of murders and violence, while at the same time, portraying him as something of a hero, constructing major portions of this transcontinental railroad.

By the end of the series, he was finished with this immense project, and was offered a position in 1870s Washington. Bohannan carried in his soul the memory of all his sins over the years of this project, and knows he wants nothing to do with Washington. On a whim, he walks out of a Washington Saturday evening gathering, and sees a church. He goes in and sees a confessional, and a priest is hearing confessions there. He obviously knows nothing of the Sacrament of Confession. He decides to try this thing called confession, and goes in. When the priest opens the screen for him to start his confession, he is tongue tied, and has no idea where to begin. He has no words about where to begin about all those shadows from his past, all those things he is filled with regret about.

Nonetheless, he was there, and he knew why he was there. However, it was too much for words, there having been too many sins for him to know where to start. The priest tries to help him get started. Still nothing. Finally the priest offers a few words of forgiveness for him, telling him of the mercy and forgiveness of the Lord, the priest knowing that it was going to have to be his words alone that could open this man to God's forgiveness.

It was enough. Bohannan heard him, said, "Thank you," got up and left both the confessional and Washington with a new heart in himself. Bohannan proceeds to look back to what was best in his life, and to set out to find it again, emboldened by those few words of the confessor.

Sacred Moments

Whoever wrote that final passage of the television series knew that moment of a person's life. He must have, or he could not have portrayed it so authentically.

Funny how that works in us. Just a quiet moment can turn us on a dime, a moment hidden from anyone, just yourself and the Lord. It catches you, and moves your heart, whatever the moment might be—forgiveness, a sense of being touched by the Savior, lifted out of this world somehow, leaving you breathless and in awe at what God is doing.

These moments exist in the Mass, perhaps more than at any other time. In precisely an empty moment, there is a voice. In exactly a thoughtless few seconds, a thought of someone you have loved appears. At just the right time, there is an awareness of the who and the why of your life. You kneel down after Communion, and you know what you need to do. You are listening carelessly to the reading of the Gospel, and you wake up to what God has been trying to tell you. There is a line in a homily, despite being one the priest has not really thought through, and it speaks exactly to your needs.

Spoken in Silence

This is the bread of the Eucharist, received as if in secret, wrapped in the silence of the Mass, caught in the net of your awareness. This is the exact same silence that underlies and is the bedrock of the Mass, and it is happening to you just as you are. Often there are no words for what you have received. The Eucharist passes silently and quietly into your soul, to form and guide the part of you that is deepest, the part of you that had been given, placed in you when God created you, waiting for this moment to be unveiled in your own consciousness.

In Communion, the voice of the Lord is silence. This is in keeping of the silence at the center of the cross, when Christ's absolute final moment is a word spoken beyond words, and the response of the Father is a word spoken beyond words—to and about us. Hearing the voice of the Lord is usually a gift from the silence around us. We get lost in it, we stroll around inside that silence, as it were, observing our lives and our challenges from the prospective of Christ and our Father in heaven. In our minds, we often know what to do next, without having to hear a voice or having someone speak to us. In Christ, in the Eucharist, in the Mass, we just know! This is how God speaks, camouflaged in silence, without words, in a whisper of absolute quiet.

The Holy Spirit

It is said that the Holy Spirit is the Love between the Father and the Son, a love so deep that it is alive and equal to both the Father and the Son. Thus, every time we connect in spirit to the central moment, the union of the Son and the Father in the stillness of the Eucharist, the Holy Spirit is released to us. That Holy Spirit then dwells within us to form and shape us in the image of the Son of God.

Just as we call down the Holy Spirit to consecrate the bread and wine into the Body and Blood of Christ, then too we should note, with great awareness, that the Holy Spirit is also called down upon us as well. It is precisely the Holy Spirit that touches us in the celebration of the Mass, that awakens us, enlivens our spirits, and moves us to both understand and to change who we are to conform more to the image of Jesus Christ, our redeemer.

I am always amazed by the hiddenness that exists in the Mass. The world has no idea, no awareness as to what is happening deep within the celebration of the Mass. The secret is available to any who would choose to access it. The mystery is right there in front of the world, and they can't see it. The Mass is filled with riches beyond belief, if you know Christ living deep within your heart.

The world watches us Sunday after Sunday and parish after parish, gathered in numbers, filling the parking lots, streaming into Mass. Surely they must wonder why it is that we do this. What is it that can be such a draw? Even were they to attend, they might miss it.

Of course, if there is no open heart to the Person of Christ in the person attending, if a person is not open to the invitation of Christ to turn his life over to Him, then the Mass seems irrelevant and obtuse, or worse, meaningless and a waste of time. But to us who have met the risen Christ, and who know that He walks with us, hidden but truly present to us, the Mass remains an event without equal anywhere in this world.

30. Identity and Our Souls

> The truth is that only in the mystery of the incarnate Word does the mystery of man take on light. For Adam, the first man, was a figure of Him Who was to come, namely Christ the Lord. Christ, the final Adam, by the revelation of the mystery of the Father and His love, fully reveals man to man himself and makes his supreme calling clear. It is not surprising, then, that in Him all the aforementioned truths find their root and attain their crown.
> *Gaudium et Spes*, Section 22

Our soul is often compared to a house. Why, I don't know, maybe it's just a natural analogy. However, let's try that out as a kind of thought experiment.

Sigmund Freud probably never wrote about the soul. I think there was no room for a soul in his atheistic perspective. However, he had a lot to say about the ego. Not quite the same thing as the soul, I know.

Freud and the Self

One of the ways to describe the human person as Freud might have seen it would be to describe it as a house. The superego is in the attic, dragging out all the rules and history and cultural demands on the ego, and the id is in the basement, railing about primal needs and proclaiming the irrational beneath everything.

The poor ego is squished into a kind of crawl space, in between, on the main floor, fighting for some breathing space between these other two parts of his humanity, almost as if the first floor were compressed and concealed in the fight between the superego and the id, between the attic and the basement. Not our image of the human person, but not a bad description of the person in a godless world, a self that's almost fugitive in an incomprehensible and unyielding universe.

Adam and the Self

Another model of the soul would be that of the human person without Christ. This too could symbolically be a house. Here the soul of the person seems as if it were a house constructed from a badly-folded blueprint. The cornerstone's out of kilter, leaving the floor askew, the walls deviating from a plumb line, doorframe ajar so that the doors don't quite close, with a roof that in some places doesn't quite join the walls that support it.

This is basically what original sin has done to the human soul. Nothing is quite right, everything is out of sync. The cornerstone is bad, so therefore is everything else about it. Not ruined completely, but awkward to live within. At times we have all tried to live in this house. Basically it ends up being a place of considerable pain, because nothing works right for very long.

This image says why it's no-go, humanly speaking, why we fight with each other, how we become estranged and are hurt by one another. Often the outcome is simply an accumulation of little things, all of which are not quite as they ought to be.

Will and Understanding Define the Soul

Then there is a classic definition of the soul. It is not a house, not a thing even. The soul, that spiritual component of ourselves, is composed of two parts. The first is the will, the second, intellect. It is ourselves, brought down to the basics of our spiritual self.

Some would use the term "reason" to describe the second part of the soul, but in this age, reason has so many overtones of the will imbedded within it, and thus suggesting, not incorrectly, an autonomy of the will over reason within the soul.

However, it seems better to use the word "understanding," a more passive term, suggesting that the truth lives independent of what the will wants, and the intellect allows the truth to rise above as an independent source of what it is that defines who we are and what we want, from where we have come, and to where we are going. Understanding allows the truth to reign, quite apart from our volition.

The Soul and Its Yes

Our will, however, is that part of our soul that allows us in freedom to respond to God's call to us. It had to be this way, otherwise we would not freely say yes to God's invitation. The book of Genesis describes this twofold makeup of us in a simple little phrase: "Then God said: Let us make human beings in our image, after our likeness" (Genesis 1:26).

One wonders why God seemingly speaks of image as something different from likeness. Once I heard the explanation that we are made in the image of God from the very beginning, but likeness comes later, suggesting we only take on the likeness of God when we respond with a yes to God, a selfless, humble yes.

The yes completes the image of God within us. If that is the case, the will in us is the part that is absolutely vital to our oneness with the Lord. This completion is not done with the power of reason but with the power of the will on our part, where we turn totally toward our Father in heaven by means of our yes to Christ. That yes is an act of love toward Christ, whole and complete. What is more, the yes of the will precedes our understanding.

The Consequences of Our Yes to Christ

At that point, in a yes, our soul is turned totally toward Christ, and toward our Father in heaven, and we are whole for the first time. This is the point where we become a new creation, have new life in us, are awakened to who it is we truly are. The cornerstone falls exactly into place, and the dimensions of the house of the soul are aligned completely toward discipleship with Christ, making us children of God.

I've also heard it said that our yes to Christ is what brings the total picture of our creatureliness into focus, that our yes to Christ is what electrifies, if you will, our understanding, carrying us to hidden vistas that can only be seen with the eyes of faith, the realm of mystery at the center of all things sacred and divine. This yes to Christ is the lens of our understanding. The choice comes first, the knowledge afterward.

Not that this yes is ever easy to hold on to. The minute we think we have got it definitively, we seem to lose the thrust of that yes. We are still victims of the fall of Adam and Eve. Fragments of that experience of those first parents cling to us. Especially in this era of secularism, where everyone defines themselves as a little god on their own, we live always on the edge of losing this likeness to Christ.

This lens, the yes, clarifies for us what it means that Christ died for us on the cross. We can see clearly the immensity of His yes to the Father, done in total selflessness. He couldn't have gone any further than He did in His total abandonment; it was limitless. Likewise when we look at the Father, His was also an absolute yes to His Son, and to us, beyond which it was not possible to go.

Our yes is a paltry little thing in comparison, yet is pointed in the right direction. All along, it needed the help of the Holy Spirit to be articulated. In the end, though, it gives us our likeness to God.

The Yes that Defines the Mass

This yes also defines for us the central moment of the Mass, where we have the opportunity to join whatever yes we can muster to the absolute yes between the Father and the Son. We are picked up in our weakness and are joined to this moment of exchange between the Son and His Father, catching as it were, the coattails of Christ's self-offering. Clearly our yes is quite beyond our capabilities. No one does a yes on his or her own, rather it is always in Christ that we solidify our yes. Every act of receiving the Eucharist binds the yes of Christ to ours, and ours to His. Our souls change when we are living in Christ. In Christ there is an order and simplicity that is absent from this world. We sense it in the Mass itself.

It is only in this context that our understanding completely kicks in. With a yes to Christ, we begin to understand who we are and why we are here. Our lives take on meaning beyond our expectations. Our lives, simple as they are, become a rich field of blessings and awarenesses in that yes. We understand things we couldn't comprehend before. We end up able to live with the human and sinful imperfections of ourselves, others, and those in the Church.

In the same way then, our ability to love God as we ought falls into place for us. Once we center our hearts on the knowledge and understanding of the love that the Father has had for us, then we acquire the gift of loving our God in return.

Yes and the Church

Often, it happens that we object to a teaching of the Church, or a stand of our bishop or Holy Father. Yet, when seen in the context of our yes to Christ, that objection pales in importance. As a result, we end up leaving our destiny or our struggles in the hands of the one to whom we have said yes. It is the love of Christ that is the engine of our faith, and we become capable of the sacrificial lifestyle that can only come from Christ. The Church falls into place within that love of Christ.

This yes changes our perspective on marriage and family. We can see more deeply into the one we love, and as a result can sacrifice more generously for our partner. As a result, as a husband and wife, we are able to say yes to another child.

We gain the strength to be generous with the goods of the earth; now we can afford to help the poor in new and deeper ways, knowing that the river of abundance flows best when we avoid hoarding it or trying to possess it for ourselves alone. In our hearts we can know now that there is always enough of the goods of this world, because we are in the hands of the Lord, who will provide sufficiently for us. All this flows from the yes to Christ, and from His subsequent love.

To live in Christ also redefines justice in our hearts, and calls us to respond to the evils of our times. Only in Christ can we see clearly the pathways open to respond to these evils that so surround us. It is not what we are within ourselves, but rather what we become in Christ that keeps us on the road to justice in our times, and enables us to endure the opposite, injustice.

Finally, in Christ, our identity comes into syncopation with what the Father in heaven designed for us from the beginning. Identity apart from Christ becomes complicated and very difficult. In Christ, we know exactly who we are, why we have come into existence, and how we are to live. We become capable of self-sacrifice. Ego ceases to be the keystone of who we are, Christ is. We can do without, for those we love. We can become humble servants of the good of this world. We truly become "persons" when we live in Christ, no longer ciphers, unsure of who we are.

We began this chapter talking about the house of our soul. The fact is that the real house of our soul is in Christ, or rather maybe that our soul and Christ have become one, and then there is only one house that we are united in, and it is Trinitarian.

31. The Choice We Have

The Lord Jesus, on the night he was handed over, took bread, and, after he had given thanks, broke it and said, "This is my body that is for you. Do this in remembrance of me." In the same way also the cup, after supper, saying, "This cup is the new covenant in my blood. Do this, as often as you drink it, in remembrance of me." For as often as you eat this bread and drink the cup, you proclaim the death of the Lord until he comes.
1 Corinthians 11:23-26

One of the experiences I have had as a priest is hearing confessions in different cultures. When I was a Maryknoll associate missioner in Korea, I had had enough time there to learn the language somewhat, so I began to hear confessions. The easiest place to start was with children's confessions, and I often had that privilege during my time there.

Because it was easier for me at first, I would give the same penance to each kid coming for confession. However, I soon learned from the children. They would come and say, "How come you gave the same penance to me that you gave to others?"

The issue was that Korean culture was vertical in makeup, a kind of ladder where each person was at a different step than anyone else. Thus, your penance, like your sins, ought to be unique to your rank. So to speak, each one should be different from any other. It might have been age or rank in family, or grade level in school, or even what sins were confessed, despite the fact that most of their sins were almost identical.

Their identity was pinned to whatever place they occupied in the ladder. The children understood who they were by what their rank was, and each was different from others. That was their way of identity in such a Confucian context, unlike Americans who would assume that they were somebody because they were on a horizontal plane, equal to everyone else.

It was a wonderful window into both cultures for me. Identity was arrived at in very different ways between the two cultures, even if it is something of an imperfect comparison.

Person in Our Times

Since that time, I have had a keen interest in what it is for our culture that makes an individual a person. It is something like a last frontier for us who are American. Who am I? What is it that makes me a person? What do I want to be? Am I a brand that I can change at will? Can I remake who I am according to the situation? Does it even matter? Am I to be defined by my sins or failures?

I sense that there is a lot of struggle with these kinds of questions here in this culture, especially given the expectation that we have to define ourselves in order for our lives to have meaning, often trying to do so without any reference to a God above. This is a culture unlike any other in history, as today all options are open to define ourselves. We often try to define our lives in terms of education or profession. We used to define ourselves by the work that we did, except that now even that has become unstable. We often don't have marriage anymore, or children to say who we are. We can even redefine ourselves in terms of gender, something that has now become a human right, somehow pulled out of midair.

Person, without Christ

Basically the problem is mostly related to the empty container of secularism. There is nothing there for a person to take hold of to define oneself. Alone in an uncreated, silent universe, isolated and unnecessary to this world or anyone in it, it takes a lot of effort to be someone, to be a person, someone more than a number or a cipher. It is a kind of race against death to be someone at all, because "this" is all there is. The past is not important, nor is the future, only this now that I have in the world.

The pressure to make ourselves into someone significant is immense, especially when so much of what this world is seems ephemeral, a fantasy, or a vain hope. Such emptiness puts great pressure on marriage and family to be more than what they can be by themselves. On top of it all, there is no intrinsic meaning to this world in secularism, only what the individual can create.

I have just described a secular world free of any divinity. There is no footing here for them, nothing to hold on to. It is truly an empty container, filled to the brim with nothingness. In this kind of world we are irrelevant. Cremation is a good symbol for the secular world we live in. Ashes, spread and forgotten. No grave to visit. Just gone. Didn't matter anyway whether we were here or not. No wonder suicide has become more common.

There is so much sadness about a postmodern world devoid of divinity, so much pointlessness.

Our Identity in Christ

Our situation, however, is different. One of the major parts of our faith is identity. In our faith, we do not define ourselves. We become one with Christ, and our identity takes shape from and with Him, who it is that completes and fulfills us in ways beyond our fondest human dreams. He is the keystone and we are the arch. Without Him, we are just a pile of rocks.

Christ is the keystone of our identities. It seems that God, when He created us, left out the key building block of who and what we are, and left that for Christ His Son to complete within us. Apart from Christ, we wander around in place and time, wondering what it is that we are missing.

Magnets in Search of Union

Here's an analogy that might work. When I was a kid, maybe five or six, my father gave me a couple of industrial magnets, throwaways from a manufacturing project. They were very powerful. In the hands of a six year old, I had little control over them. They would clomp onto whatever metal was nearby, a stove or a metal pot. If I put one into our kitchen junk drawer, every piece of metal, nail, paper clip, old key, and what have you, would get pulled out of the drawer.

I look back and I see that half of a magnet set is a bit like us when we are on our own. It's what makes us addictive, grabbing a hold of whatever is nearest to hold on to, or to find our identity.

Since my father had given me two of them, I found that the most powerful arrangement was to put them together north to south, and south to north. They seemed designed for that. When I brought them together they would snap to each other, they were home, double in holding power over each separately! This is a pretty good analogy of ourselves. We are one half of a set of magnets, clomping onto whatever is nearest. We can barely control ourselves, even on a good day.

However, when we are brought in touch with the power of Christ, we are home. We are complete. We know what we were made for. This is how the Father's plan for us was put in motion. We are only who we are totally when we are connected to Jesus Christ. Then we know exactly what and who we are, and where we fit in this world. We are exactly like that set of magnets joined to each other, Christ and us.

First Days of Christianity

I long for the days of the early Church, to be able to have witnessed the first converts to the faith in the time of the Apostles, on the journeys of Paul, despite the fact that I have seen many in my own lifetime. I would have loved to have sat there in a corner watching those who were slaves and chattel of the Roman Empire discover that in Christ they took on a whole new identity, that they found themselves persons of infinite worth, loved immensely by Christ and His Father in heaven. I have a hunch that they were stunned over and over again about what they had become in Christ. This was so much so that they were then willing to die for Christ, for what He had given to them spiritually.

They understood sacrifice as He had taught them by means of the cross. They could not keep their mouths shut about this awesome miracle that had happened in their souls. The presence of the risen Christ changed their lives, their marriages, their whole purpose in life. They knew, from that moment on, exactly who they were.

Those who had found themselves in Christ, when they heard the Gospel proclaimed in their midst, understood exactly what many of the parables were about. They found ones that were about the conversion process, and the change that it instilled within their lives. They got the parable of the sower. They quickly understood it was about what had happened to them, the hundredfold yield. They understood the parable of the buried treasure and the companion parable of the pearl of great price. They were it, the treasure and the pearl. They had been found by the Lord.

They got the story of the prodigal son, loved by the father, even after a sinful life. They knew it was they themselves whom the father threw a robe around, and put a ring on their fingers, and declared a banquet, because they had been dead and were also brought back to life. They knew it was about them being found by God's love.

When they heard about the miracles of the Gospel, about hearing or seeing, or standing up and walking, they intuitively saw those things happening spiritually within their daily lives. They understood a new way of seeing what was invisible. The miracle of the man born blind, in John's Gospel, was who they were. They could hear a new message of a truth beyond anything in this world. They got the part about the cripple at the pool of Bethesda, cured by Christ. He was them! Everything was a window into the change that had taken place within their souls, highlighting the miracle of who and what they had become.

The key piece in their conversion was undoubtedly that central moment when out of obedience to His Father, Christ gave His life in exchange for them on the cross. In finality, that cross consecrated everything about who they had become.

Those first Christians understood that arresting moment of total giving by Christ's dying, a moment that alone could have restored dignity and worth to humanity, and that now they were who they were because of that moment. That moment was then cemented in place by their celebration of the Mass, done in a form as we do today, with every celebration of the Eucharist, furthering and deepening that identity. They knew theologically what it was to be "person."

Identity and the Mass

This brings us back to the present times. I don't doubt whenever we celebrate the Eucharist that most faithful share somehow that same sense of identity that the first Christians discovered. It is precisely in those moments of the Mass that we most know who we are, what we are worth, and what dignity Christ has prepared for us in our own souls. How could we not, in the moment of Communion.

Perhaps we could find our Christian identity without the Mass, maybe in the Bible, maybe in love for the poor. However we have at hand the very central moment of our salvation, of all of history actually, whenever we celebrate the Mass, a beacon of light to our soul.

Our identity is locked in by the reception of the Body and Blood of Christ within us. Each time we receive the Eucharist we turn ourselves over to Him, we know that He completes in us the creation that the Father placed within us, waiting to be opened up in Christ. That conversion I referred to in the early days of the Church is now ongoing in us who celebrate the mysteries of the Eucharist.

Our Choice, Either/Or

How tragic these times we live in, when divorced from the only true source of identity that is in Christ, every vestige of faith is either jettisoned or forgotten. The empty container of secularism knows no savior, no redeemer, no enduring presence, no source of love beyond the horizontal. How can they know who they are? What is an identity in so empty a space?

The Army had a saying, "Be all that you can be," and then didn't have in itself what it would take to reveal what it is you could be. There is no answer to the mystery of self, apart from Jesus Christ.

So, here is our choice in this postmodern world: either the Blood of Christ in the chalice, or that empty container filled with nothingness. It is no wonder that when a person sits down and reflects carefully, they can feel the yearning within themselves for the chalice of salvation. We are so constructed. The Blood of the Chalice calls us to become one with Him who died for our sins. The empty container beckons us to sever the bond that God has placed within us, to go on, unhampered by any boundaries. Here lies the choice of the modern world within which we live.

32. The Milieu in Which We Live

> "Who are these wearing white robes,
> and where did they come from?"
> I said to him, "My lord, you are the one who knows."
> He said to me, "These are the ones who have survived the time of great distress; they have washed their robes and made them white in the blood of the Lamb."
> Revelation 9:13-14

As a people of faith in Jesus Christ, what have we got, what is it that we have? More so than any other age, we need the answer to that question.

Ours is an age of secularism, a world described as postmodern, an age like an empty container, filled with nothingness, in a universe that is silent and unyielding of any purpose or meaning whatsoever. For this strange age, there is no God, no Jesus Christ. There are no limits. The age is awash in freedom.

My thesis has been this: secularism is less than a philosophy, not so much a code as it is a milieu, an environment we have to live in, virtually invisible to us in our minds, almost like the water the fish swims in, so pervasive that the fish is unaware of the water's existence. For the vast majority of us, we do not own this secularism. We have been living in it for so long that we are unaware of its existence, blind to its consequences.

Our Illumination in the Eucharist

However, along with that context, I would contend that the Eucharist, the Mass we celebrate, contains within itself the depth of mystery which can make secularism visible in all its details for us. The Mass, understood in depth, can pull away the mask of secularism of our age, unveil the true shape of the postmodern world in which we are living, but ordinarily can't see.

We need clarity on the Mass, not a shallow, pedestrian understanding of the Mass, but one in which we take ownership of the very heart of mystery that is contained within the silence and ritual of the Mass. Once we allow the Blood of the Chalice to inform and complete us, we will never be comfortable with just the empty container of secularism.

The depth of the Eucharist can illuminate the era in which we live. If we focus correctly on what it is we have in the Mass, we will be astounded that we were even trying to live partially in the secular world, in the empty, inverted, alternative universe of Satan.

This world has snuck up on us who are Catholic, especially in America. We had come to expect full membership in this culture, only to find out that we are experiencing an ongoing series of compromises in order to be a part of what has now become secular. We thought we had made it as American Catholics, only to find out that the ground under our feet shifted, and once more we are on the outside looking in.

On top of that, the usual answers don't work very well today, and we find ourselves in an unusual state of confusion about spiritual matters.

When we argue in support of what the Church teaches, we get nowhere. When we fall back on God or Christ, we get laughter from beyond. No one around us wants to deal with ethics or morality anymore. They can't, because that only can come from above! Everything is allowed. We fit into this culture about as well as the Amish do.

Thus we have to ask, what have we got within our faith to help us in these times?

The Constant and the Variable

Let's take the part of secularism first. We have to live with secularism day in and day out. My intent has not been to attack secularism, even though I think it is a fair, easy target. I have no interest in focusing on an apologetic approach to this postmodern world. In the end, the subject of what I write here is not the secularism of our world. Secularism is what it is. Secularism is a constant, not a variable. It is not necessary to center our attention on secularism, but rather to address our full minds and hearts on what is central to our faith, and what tools can infuse and complete us in that faith.

No, the real variable among the tools that we have, in fact, the ultimate tool we have, is in the core of the Mass. The Eucharist is the variable in these essays, not secularism, even though we have to give that secularism some space.

The Mass is the part that has inexhaustible potential for us. The endless depth of the Mass, as it reflects the expansive moment of the dying and rising of Jesus Christ—all this is at the nexus of eternity, manifested in the present moment of the presence of Christ with us. That moment flows, start and finish, from the one central moment of the cross, revealed in the Mass. The more we comprehend the Mass, the better to deal with the secularism of our times.

While I understand the limitations of secularism, I do not discount that it is a force in our times. It has roots back through more than four centuries, and has found its strongest proponents today ever. In dealing with it, we ought not approach our faith around the edges or on the periphery. We need to bring our best faith to bear on this generation.

The Leaky Boat of Secularism

This secularism we live amidst, this empty container is a kind of leaky boat to set sail on. The transcendent has a way of seeping into the lives of the secular. The transcendent ways of our Christianity are an affront to the immanence of secularism, our faith always suggesting meaning and purpose, causality and intent from everything around us in the universe. Such truths can't help but to leak alarmingly into the consciousness of the secular!

The postmodern world we live in allows for no meaning or purpose, and as a result, has no explanation for what is happening in our times. Secularism is clueless when it comes to explanations to the endless issues of our times.

Here's a prime example: recently we witnessed the mass murder of 59 people and the wounding of hundreds more in Las Vegas, Nevada. The shooter, wealthy and talented, was in a hotel room at the Mandalay Bay hotel some 30 floors above a rock concert. His death ended the massacre. The media went into its usual frenzy, seeking to find out why this man had done such a despicable crime, wondering what motive he could have had. In the end they could come up with nothing, straws in the wind.

This is precisely what the media has come up with regarding other recent shootings such as the Parkland, Florida, shooting at Marjory Stoneman Douglas High School, the Orlando nightclub shooting, the Virginia Tech shooting, or the Sandy Hook Elementary School shooting.

When all is said and done, no explanation satisfies. This is simply because nothing vertical, nothing theological, nothing spiritual is there in secularism to deal with such madness.

The Source of Evil in our Times

Why no good answers? The media centers itself in the secular realm, looking to psychology, or to science for an explanation. Because the secular world separated itself from anything theological, there is nothing accountable for what is happening today in this world. As a result, the media looks simply to the individual who has perpetrated these atrocities, to ask what went wrong with this individual. They can find no satisfying explanation.

Perhaps the source of this evil lies more not with the individual, but rather with the context within which individuals live. In fact, three elements of the environment show a whole different context of what has happened over and over in our times, something that the media seems not to comprehend. These three represent a perfect storm today in the break up of values.

- First, the transcendental is gone. This is an environment that lives in the absence of God, and in denial of the presence of Jesus Christ. This denial leaves the culture without any guiding morality, with basically no right and wrong that can be grounded anywhere. Anything is possible, anything can be done in the extreme mind of those without Christian morality. Were Christ to have been acknowledged as present, the context of the environment would be vastly different. However, today, there is no place for Christ.

- Secondly, we have generations of individuals angry because they can't have it all, because their right to entitlement has been thwarted. These have followed the thoughts that occur nationally, that everyone has a right to whatever they want, and to be prevented from getting it makes them victims unfairly. Thus, there are many people around who carry grudges, want revenge, and are going to make someone pay the price for their not getting what they think they are entitled to. This anger is pervasive today; many see themselves as victims of an unfair and unjust culture, and that justifies virtually anything.
- Thirdly, there is support for putting guns in every possible hand, in every family and every home. There is no limit to the guns, even automatic rifles, machine pistols, and submachine guns. If you will pardon the exaggeration, maybe even bazookas would be allowed in the hands of any person these days, whatever their condition, age, responsibility or training.

So in the end, there is an absence of transcendentals, coupled with an almost nationwide anger, and the presence of an endless array of weapons of revenge. Once again, the perfect storm!

A Theological Void

The total absence of Christ in the context of secularism is an absence without parallel. No wonder an explanation for such violence is impossible, because in a secular world, there is no Christ to begin with. As a result there is nothing theological or transcendental with which to orient our lives, nothing spiritual to guide us in our weakness and sinfulness, no redeemer, no one to draw out the goodness inherent within us, apart from our faith in Christ. Hence the postmodern world is left isolated and without a compass to navigate the terrain of this age, wandering interminably from one incomprehensible crisis event to another.

Our ability to cope with and to prevent or endure the evil of these times requires the presence of Christ. We would at least know from where such evil arises. There would have to be something theological or spiritual in order to answer the media's probing of "what went wrong in the latest mass shooting." It all suggests a "cultural" disease, not just in the individual, but in the very context of existence today.

How can this secular world look at the subject of evil in our midst? This is a transcendental topic, and it opens the door to where goodness comes from, how evil is the absence of goodness, or why such a "thing" as evil might exist, even though it is apart from God's creation. To repeat, here we are looking at Satan's inverted, alternative universe.

A secular culture has nothing that can give meaning or purpose or destiny to a life. The negation of Christ's presence with us in this culture means that anger and violence can run rampant. The emptiness of secularism leaves a void that can't be filled. We know that the void is connected to the absolute denial of Christ or of God in our midst, who alone can give us the power to deal with such realities.

Coping with the Evil of Our Times

Curiously, we, of faith, do not have the answers to what is happening in our times. Yet we do have something remarkable that enables us to cope with the mystery of evil in our midst, something that allows us to hold in our hearts the meaning of our lives. That something is the presence of Jesus Christ. His presence gives us few answers materially, but often it is only the oneness with Christ that enables us to deal with the evil and contradictions of our times spiritually. That presence is most manifest in the Eucharist, and from there we carry it in our hearts throughout the days and nights. The depth of this presence of Christ is limitless to us, reaching all the way to eternity, and as far as the shattered gates of hell.

What No Longer Works for Us

It used to be that one could live on the margins of faith, pretty much coasting along without much effort, and you wouldn't lose your faith. You could exist at the margins, almost for a lifetime, and still find your way home to the faith by the end. You didn't have to take it too seriously. Family and spouse would sustain you, or Catholic schools would give you enough that you could "get by" as a Catholic. You wouldn't lose your faith, even if it were minimal.

Often, that faith was not tested. Occasional Sunday Masses, especially at Easter and Christmas would have seemed enough for some. Confession, if you had to! You could pick up enough of the faith through your parents.

Those days are long gone. Now, thanks to the media and the World Wide Web, our children begin to live in a godless environment even as ten year olds. They have this totally secular environment, and may have seen nothing else, unless someone takes them aside and teaches them about the presence of Christ in their heart.

Often, parents even lack the power to prevent this absence of faith that the culture is teaching their children, and that grows in them virtually unnoticed. This loss of faith today is a huge source of pain for many families who have seen their children grow up and lose their way.

Faith in the 21st Century

Today, faith has to be intentional, not habitual or serendipitous. Today, each disciple of Christ has to have been converted, turned completely to Christ. There is no alternative. The community has lost its power to draw people along the way. There is no alternative to meeting Jesus Christ, setting aside everything else in this world, and saying "yes" to him with one's whole heart. This step is not for an elite, not for the exceptional person, not having to be a monk in a monastery or a religious hidden away in a convent. This step of total commitment to Christ has to move us one by one, or it is no-go today.

We do have a remarkable resource, however. Buried deep within the Eucharist, the Mass, is everything we need to access both the presence of Christ, as well as the forgiveness of sins, and the restoration of our nature to what our Father in heaven has placed within us.

Why settle for less? We need to go right to the heart of our Christianity, and take ahold of what is deepest and richest about what and who we are today. It is all hidden in plain sight in the celebration of the Eucharist, the Mass that has been passed on to us from the Last Supper and the crucifixion of our Savior. It is the ultimate defining moment of all of history, and it is ours.

In plain sight, yes, but visible only with the eyes of faith. The Mass experienced with the eyes of faith aligns our lives to the sacred and to its mysteries. This is the primary tool we need to deal with these times.

The Illumination of Our Times

However, we have to get to its absolute core! Once we find the depth of the Mass and the Eucharist, once we experience the love of Christ manifested there, this secular environment lights up for us like a neon sign, as to what kind of environment we are really confronting.

The best of our faith lies at the very center of things: the moment of the cross of Christ, gathered together in the Mass through the centuries, where all time ceases, where angels are ascending and descending between our altars and that in heaven. If only we would understand what it is that we have in the wondrous gift we have in the Mass and the Eucharist that negates this incipient environment.

It's a simple choice today: either it will be the Blood of the Chalice that enlivens us, or it's the empty container of our postmodern world.

33. The Need to Stay Awake

"Awake, O sleeper, and arise from the dead, and Christ will give you light." Watch carefully then how you live, not as foolish persons but as wise, making the most of the opportunity, because the days are evil.
Ephesians 5:14

In 1956 there was a black and white film that became a kind of cult classic. The title was the *Invasion of the Body Snatchers*. The storyline was that there were aliens present in our midst, and that when a person slept, a pod encased the body and turned the person into a kind of zombie. Once people understood the risk, they tried everything to avoid sleep, but in the end had to succumb to sleep, thus becoming victims to the invaders.

The film became a kind of parable for modern times, and has hung around for decades. One interpretation focused on communism of the 1950s, perceiving that such was somehow similar to the storyline of the film, that if we didn't pay attention we would be lost to this undermining and pervasive philosophy. Another interpretation was that the story was an analogy of the growing alcoholism and drug use of the late 20th century. This was not far from the reality of such addictions.

Here, I can see the film's application analogous to the world of secularism in which we live. These postmodern times require us to remain awake to the challenges of faith that they represent.

The Price of Faith Today

The state capital of Minnesota has the saying over its entrance, often quoted, "Eternal vigilance is the price of liberty." The issue of secularism has a particular vulnerability for us who are disciples of Christ, for us who are Catholic in these times. The fact is that secularism lulls us to sleep, promising coexistence, implying that we can have it all, both the secular and faith at the same time.

This secularism asks us to make a few, simple compromises to how we live, adjustments to the truths we hold, so we can then participate fully in the wonderful, self-fulfilling existence of these times, in an easier, more gratifying world to which we would then be entitled. Once we examine this participation in detail, it begins to look like the "nose of the camel under the tent," requiring more and more from us to the point where all we have left in our faith is a shadow of what true faith really is.

The most toxic portion of secularism centers on children, marriage, and family. Its primary instrument in this is induced inattentiveness to each of these three things. We simply fall asleep about how fundamental the formation of our children is, how to protect our marriages, and what the absolute place of the family is in our discipleship toward Christ. We become zombie Catholics, as it were, hypnotized and tone-deaf to what is happening in our midst, trusting and compliant to the forces that underlie this secularism.

We turn our children over to the public school system, somehow expecting that the system would remain neutral and balanced. We open our children to the Internet, buy them cell phones, and thus connect them to a peer culture over which there is no control. We sanction every kind of activity, even at the middle school and junior high school levels. We just don't pay attention, thinking it is a safe and harmless environment for our youth.

Of course, even if nothing is intended to hurt our youth, the question remains, "Who is in charge?" The sociologists? The media? Planned Parenthood? Congress?

Ultimately no one is, if parents and family are not! Anything goes, then. As a result, in such a context we can expect almost anything to arise.

The culture reduces marriage to "a piece of paper," a contract. Commitment is not really lifelong. In addition, nor is openness to children intrinsic to marriage anymore. It is not just gay marriage, it is any kind of marriage that the culture finds arbitrary. There is an unstated indifference to any type of marriage whatsoever.

The Consequences of Secularism for Us

The net result of living in an environment of secularism is a kind of numbness to spiritual matters. After a time, given that we haven't taken our faith seriously enough, we become progressively more ignorant of what is invisible to the eye. Our conscience flattens, sin no longer a part of our awareness. We become disenchanted with our Christian identity. We don't really know who Christ is.

Part of the evidence of this numbness of spirit is shown by our continued inability to understand the Scriptures. We don't know where to begin with the Word of God. We sit silently at Mass through the readings and the Gospel, wondering what any of that has to do with our lives. Saint Paul's words are a cipher. The parables seem unconnected to our experience. The words of Jesus don't move us in any way. Often, we have never been converted, turned toward Christ, never yielding up our spirit to Him that He might overcome our incessant egos and selfishness. We don't know where to start when it comes to living our faith. We are, in the end, perfect candidates for the secularism of the postmodern world.

Secularism preys on the weakness of our faith, on our never having gotten beyond the first steps of becoming a true disciple of Christ. It can smell a victim from a mile away who has never owned much of anything about Christ, our heavenly Father, or the Church. This person could dabble in oriental religions, self-help programs, or put their faith in yoga, endlessly trying out the dead ends of the past.

This has been Satan's best move in all of history. He has operated not by confrontation, but rather by subtle innuendo, by allowing the level of attentiveness to fall on the premise that all is well, that all this will work to the entitlement of every American today.

The proof of Satan's role, that the further we get into this new, postmodern era, is the fact that the secular is turning coercive and even violent. The seemingly attractive and innocent secularism is morphing into Satan's alternative, inverted universe. The subtle innuendo is gradually being replaced by a set of requirements that we are to be in compliance with. Those who choose not to live in this new, subjectively limitless universe are now frequently labeled as bigots, as violators of human rights. Needless to say, such human rights have only recently been formulated arbitrarily, and are now defined as requirements to participate in the culture, as if they were the consensus of the society.

We need to pay close attention to what is happening today. Secularism is more and more defined as anything but neutral. It is a code that requires participation, and will result in punishment if it is ignored or resisted.

Secularism will likely become a form of totalitarianism. It's the invasion of the body snatchers, or perhaps, the soul snatchers.

Seeing Beyond the Secular

Catholicism needs awareness of the times in which we are living. We need to see secularism for what it is, not to be impressed with it, but to understand what it does to us when we have not truly possessed Christ in our hearts.

Our faith needs to be deeply rooted in the mysteries that we celebrate, the mysteries that are contained in the Mass itself. We need to remain awake and alert to what it is we hold in our faith. We need to grasp the truth that emerges from the revelation centered on the dying and rising of Christ. His word and action needs to touch us! These mysteries in depth are the reality we need to hold. Nothing else will suffice.

Witness the way the Church has always dealt with Satan throughout history. Satan has never really been our focus. True, we have always done exorcisms when necessary. However, Satan is mostly irrelevant to who we are and what we are about. Of course, Satan hovers at the margins of our souls, but whenever we turn our focus totally on Christ, the Savior and redeemer of the world, the one who lives in our hearts, Satan diminishes in importance in our everyday lives.

It will be the same with secularism. It is not our focus as Catholics. Christ is! He is the center of the burning bush. He is the one who walks with us. He is the one before whom every knee shall bend, in the heavens, on the earth, and below. He is the one whom we meet every time we celebrate the Eucharist. He is the one we receive into our hearts when we take of His Body and Blood.

To the extent to which we center ourselves on the mystery at the heart of our faith, secularism deserves little of our energy or our concerns. This is what it means for us to stay awake in these times, not so much about the nothingness of secularism, but rather about the fulness of the mystery that lies at the heart of our faith. We have to know this secularism of our times, and understand what it is, but it does not deserve to be the center of our focus. We are not rabbits staring into the eyes of a predator. We are children of the Father, disciples of Christ, born again into life of the Spirit.

The decisive moment has already happened. Christ is risen and present as a result of the cross. We witness that moment every time we celebrate the Mass and come in contact with the Eucharist. In the Mass, when we understand the mystery within it, we stand victorious over the evil of our times.

A Partial Bibliography

One of the gifts of my life is that I have always found time to read. None of that reading makes me a theologian, but simply a parish priest who has always had a lot of questions, both about the mysteries that I have been commissioned to celebrate, and to the times in which we are living.

In all of this, I am a beginner. I think that I have only run the gamut from A to B, so to speak. I wander the halls of writings, like one overwhelmed by a mansion with its multiplicity of rooms and space, filled with knowledge, much of it well beyond my comprehension. Yet, I have been fascinated.

Here is a partial list of literature that I have found worthwhile for my journey.

- The writings of our Holy Fathers: Blessed Paul VI, Saint John Paul II, Pope Benedict XVI, and Pope Francis.

- I keep going back to the encyclical of *Humanae Vitae* of Paul VI, seen more and more as the watershed moment of modern history, demarcating the collapse of morality in the 20th century and the crisis of the Church that resulted from its unwillingness to address the issues contained within it. Nothing has been more prophetic about the world we now live in. It is still one hundred years ahead of its time.

- Read everything by Pope Benedict. He is a wonderful writer, always crystal clear with perfectly timed analogies, the best of theology.

- Ditto for Saint John Paul II! Especially on the Theology of the Body.
- Get the writings of Archbishop Charles Chaput as well. He writes well about the American Catholic experience in these times.
- I have found the writings of Urs von Balthasar to be an endless goldmine of reflections. I think him to have been the most educated man of the 20th century. Don't hesitate to dive into his volumes, the seven of *The Glory of the Lord*, the five-volume *Theo-Drama*, and the three-volume *Theo-Logic*. They will challenge the reader with its philosophical demands, but throughout holds some of the most beautiful and thought provoking theology of modern times. He has a knack for identifying those writers and theologians most significant throughout history for what best defines the deepest threads of teaching about the Church.
- There are other writers that hold insights into our times as well.

  Alasdair MacIntyre's *After Virtue: A Study in Moral Theology*

  Charles Taylor's *A Secular Age*

  Mary Eberstadt's *How the West Really Lost God: A New Theory of Secularization*

  Patrick Deneen's *Why Liberalism Failed*

  Rene Girard's *I See Satan Fall like Lightning*

  Jean-Luc Marion's *Believing in Order to See*

  Rod Dreher's *The Benedict Option*

  Brad Gregory's *The Unintended Reformation*

Again, these are often tough reading, but worth the effort. All of them speak to the times, the bizarre and secular times to which the Catholic Faith needs to respond in this 21st century.

Some Additional Notes on the Content

1. All of the quotations from Sacred Scripture are taken from the Catholic *New American Bible Revised Edition*. Fairbrother, 2018. Apple Books eBook.
2. The use of the image "the empty container of secularism" is derived from a narrower use of the word "container" that Charles Taylor's *A Secular Age* used to describe time for the secular. I used it to describe all of secularism.
3. In describing the focus of our Father toward what is good in us, there is a wonderful passage in *Theo-Logic I: Truth of the World*, near p. 116, by Hans Urs von Balthasar.
4. In describing the difference between image and likeness, there is another wonderful passage from *Theo-Drama III*, by Hans Urs von Balthasar.
5. Hans Urs von Balthasar, in *Explorations in Theology IV*, talks at length about humility as a characteristic of divinity.
6. In describing the lens that we use to see by the eyes of faith, I would recommend Jean-Luc Marion's *Believing in Order to See*. He brings much clarity to the gift of the eyes of faith.

 **About Leonine Publishers**

Leonine Publishers LLC makes fine Catholic literature available to Catholics throughout the English-speaking world. Leonine Publishers offers an innovative "hybrid" approach to book publication that helps authors as well as readers. Please visit our web site at www.leoninepublishers.com to learn more about us. Browse our online bookstore to find more solid Catholic titles to uplift, challenge, and inspire.

Our patron and namesake is Pope Leo XIII, a prudent, yet uncompromising pope during the stormy years at the close of the 19th century. Please join us as we ask his intercession for our family of readers and authors.

www.leoninepublishers.com